THE School Efficiency Series comprises about ten volumes by as many educational experts on Elementary School and Kindergarten, High School, and Vocational Instruction, Courses of Study, Organization, Management and Supervision. The series consists of monographs—with additions plainly indicated in each volume—constituting the report of Professor Hanus and his associates on the schools of New York City, but the controlling ideas are applicable as well in one public school system as in another. The series also comprises reports on other school surveys. Among the authors contributing to these volumes are Professor Paul H. Hanus, Professor of Education, Harvard University, who is also gene al editor of the series; Dr. Frank P. Bachman, Educational Expert, General Education Board, New York City; Dr. Edward C. Elliott, Director of the School of Education, University of Wisconsin; Dr. Herman Schneider, Dean of the College of Engineering, University of Cincinnati; Dr. Frank W. Ballou, Director of Promotion and Educational Measurement, Boston Public Schools; Dr. Calvin O. Davis, Assistant Professor of Education, University of Michigan; Dr. Frank V. Thompson, Assistant Superintendent of Schools, Boston; Dr. Henry H. Goddard, Director Department of Psychological Research, New Jersey Training School for Feeble-Minded Boys and Girls; Mr. Stuart A. Courtis, Supervisor of Educational Research in the Public Schools, Detroit; Dr. Frank M. McMurry, Professor of Elementary Education, Teachers College, Columbia University; Dr. Ernest C. Moore, Professor of Education, Harvard University; Dr. Ellwood P. Cubberley, Professor of Education, Leland Stanford Junior University.

SCHOOL EFFICIENCY SERIES

Education for Industrial Workers

SCHOOL EFFICIENCY SERIES
Edited by PAUL H. HANUS

Education for Industrial Workers

A Constructive Study applied to New York City

By HERMAN SCHNEIDER, Sc.D.
DEAN OF THE COLLEGE OF ENGINEERING
UNIVERSITY OF CINCINNATI

YONKERS-ON-HUDSON, NEW YORK
WORLD BOOK COMPANY
1915

Copyright, 1915, by World Book Company
All rights reserved
SES: SEIW—I

EDITOR'S PREFACE

AT the present time there is scarcely a city in the country that is not seeking an answer to the question discussed in this volume — What kinds of vocational (industrial) schools are required to meet the needs of our youth who must go to work at an early age?

Dean Schneider has long been known for his fruitful work in seeking a satisfactory answer to this question. In this book he maintains that all-day trade schools *for training prior to gainful employment* cannot alone provide the vocational training needed, because of the relatively small number of persons who can take advantage of them; that indeed in most communities they are not even possible if they are to be at all adequate in scope and equipment, owing to the great initial expense and the cost of keeping them up-to-date. Consequently, his answer is that the schools we need are schools *providing training that accompanies gainful employment* — part-time or coöperative industrial schools, and continuation schools.

His analysis of work and consequent classification of work as *energizing,* — that is, work requiring thought as well as skill, — and *enervating,* — that is, work requiring little or no thought and little or no skill, — is an illuminating introduction to his discussion of the entire subject.

Dean Schneider's answer is no mere theoretical solution of the problem of providing appropriate and accessible industrial education for the great majority of wage earners. Schools of the kind he advocates are already in successful operation in several states of the Union, some of them schools which his own persuasive and enthusiastic advocacy have brought into existence; in some of them he has himself been active as a directing force.

Editor's Preface

Coöperative and continuation schools necessarily involve the coöperation of industry and education. This coöperation is becoming increasingly possible because both industry and the school are coming to realize that neither of them alone can discharge the educational responsibilities society must discharge to its young workers, but that both together can and should discharge them in the interests of industrial and social welfare.

Dean Schneider was induced by me to undertake for New York City the study covered by this volume, when I was in charge (in 1911–12) of the Educational Aspects of the School Inquiry undertaken by the Committee on School Inquiry of the Board of Estimate and Apportionment of the City of New York. When he investigated the opportunities for the industrial education of boys and girls provided by the City of New York, he found those opportunities so insignificant in amount that it was clear that the best service he could render was to define a policy of industrial education for the city and to offer constructive suggestions for carrying that policy into effect. This he did in the report submitted to me, and by me incorporated in the report which I made to the Committee on School Inquiry. Because of the importance of Dean Schneider's report, I welcomed the opportunity to publish it, substantially unchanged, as a volume of the School Efficiency Series, and thus to render it accessible to constructive workers in the field of industrial education outside of as well as within New York City.

PAUL H. HANUS.

HARVARD UNIVERSITY.

CONTENTS

	PAGE
EDITOR'S PREFACE BY PAUL H. HANUS	vii

THE NEED OF INDUSTRIAL EDUCATION

CHAPTER
- I. THE OBJECT OF INDUSTRIAL EDUCATION 3
- II. WORK AS RELATED TO MODERN INDUSTRIAL CONDITIONS 5
- III. CLASSIFICATION OF WORK 12
- IV. INDUSTRIAL EDUCATION IN THE PUBLIC SCHOOL . . 16

THE PROBLEM IN NEW YORK CITY

- V. THE NUMERICAL SIZE OF THE PROBLEM 21
- VI. THE INDUSTRIAL SCOPE OF THE PROBLEM 23
- VII. PRESENT PLANS OF INDUSTRIAL EDUCATION 28

THE SOLUTION

- VIII. EDUCATION PRIOR TO GAINFUL EMPLOYMENT . . . 47
- IX. EDUCATION ACCOMPANYING GAINFUL EMPLOYMENT . 55
- X. THE COÖPERATIVE COURSE IN DETAIL 59
- XI. THE CONTINUATION SCHOOL IN DETAIL 67
- XII. HOW TO INAUGURATE CONTINUATION AND COÖPERATIVE SCHOOLS—COMPARATIVE ADVANTAGES OF THE TWO PLANS 71

CONCLUSIONS

- XIII. CONCLUSIONS CONCERNING INDUSTRIAL EDUCATION OF CHILDREN—IMPROVEMENTS IN PRESENT FACILITIES RECOMMENDED 79

APPENDICES

	PAGE
APPENDIX A. OCCUPATIONS OF CHILDREN IN NEW YORK CITY	85
APPENDIX B. THE NEW YORK PARENTAL SCHOOL	89
INDEX	95

The Need of Industrial Education

EDUCATION FOR INDUSTRIAL WORKERS

CHAPTER I

THE OBJECT OF INDUSTRIAL EDUCATION

THE THREE ELEMENTS DETERMINING INDUSTRIAL EFFICIENCY

INDUSTRIAL education has as its object a progressive community advancement through industrial efficiency. Industrial efficiency is determined by three mutually dependent elements — physical health, mental development, and manual dexterity.

The health element in industrial education is only slightly within the jurisdiction of the school authorities, and, except in specific instances, is outside the scope of this inquiry. It will be evident, too, that in some occupations hand skill is negligible — for example, in selling. In nearly all trades, however, it is an important factor. Generally speaking, then, we are concerned with the two elements of mental development and manual dexterity.

FUNCTION OF THE SCHOOL IN THE WAY OF SUPPLYING ELEMENTS NOT FURNISHED BY INDUSTRY

If industry itself furnished these two elements, there would be no problem of industrial education. What industry furnishes properly and adequately requires no effort on the part of the school. But, if industry emphasizes one element at the expense of another, or utterly neglects both, the school, standing for community advancement, may enter into the situation. Again, if industry in some of its phases requires a certain type of manual work which leads to mental stagnation, the public school's function would not be to initiate or to increase such manual dexterity; this would not be education. On the contrary, the school's efforts would aim to counteract the dulling effects of the work. It is obvious, then, before any constructive criticism of industrial programs now in operation or suggestions for their betterment can be formulated, that an analysis of the thing we call work, especially with reference to the mental effects of factory work under modern conditions, is necessary.

CHAPTER II

WORK AS RELATED TO MODERN INDUS-TRIAL CONDITIONS [1]

THERE is an instinct for work, but basically it is the instinct for self-preservation and self-perpetuation. Work is our individual and collective struggle for existence; and, out of the mental and physical exertion of the struggle to feed, clothe, and house us, has evolved our present state of being. The whole complex machine of commerce and industry — factory, farm, railroad, bank, office, government — has been built for production, construction, distribution, and protection. The present machine is the product of slow evolution; and the effort of the centuries to build a machine which will better cope with the problem has been the primary cause of our advance in the various activities of life. Integrity, honesty, discipline, sound health, fair dealing, respect for others' rights — these have come from the courageous assumption of one's burden of work, and the opposites of these are the results of the desire to dodge the burden.

THE NATURAL LAW OF WORK

And so we have a natural law of work, the substance of which is this: Work and you will reach a higher mental development; cease work and you will degenerate.

[1] Most of the material on *work* in this chapter (II) is taken from former papers by the writer as follows: "The University and the Day's Work," New York State Teachers' Convention, Dec., 1910; "The Public School and the Day's Work," National Child Labor Convention, March, 1911; "Community Efficiency," Commencement Address, Fitchburg, Mass., June, 1911; "An Analysis of Work," in "Lecture Notes on Some Aspects of Shop Practice," by Alex. Humphries, 1912.

The law can be established scientifically if need be, but it is not necessary, for in this case common observation, science, and religion all agree. Each of us knows he will deteriorate physically and mentally if he ceases constructive work, and history shows that this is also true of communities, of nations, and of civilizations. Our proverbs, sacred and secular, affirm it. The cycle of work to wealth, wealth to idleness, idleness to poverty, and poverty to work again, is an evidence of inefficiency following inaction. Mental and physical activity are mutually stimulating; thinking and doing are reciprocal aids.

FORMER ALLIANCE OF MENTAL TRAINING AND INDUSTRY

Mental training and industry have both been most stable when they have been most closely allied; and until comparatively recent years they have been one in fact. Under the old guild and apprentice systems, for example, the workers were trained so well in the commercial field that industrial education was not a special school problem. Work *was* education. To embark upon an apprenticeship was serious business; careful discussion preceded it and ample documentary agreements gave guarantees of execution. Industrial communities were small, and personal acquaintance fostered personal interest. Competition in skilful execution furnished a lively stimulus which led to the enthusiastic use of head and hand coördinately. Generation by generation there was a cumulative mental advancement coupled with a refinement of manual skill in constructive work. In this manner, even long before the days of formal apprenticeship, mankind grew through work.

CHANGES WITH INTRODUCTION OF FACTORY SYSTEM

But there have been two significant changes in the conditions under which work is done.

In the first place, it is only within the past two or three

generations that mankind has worked in masses within walls. For centuries mankind did self-directed work, largely in the open air. These were the farmers, the seamen, and the forest rangers. As civilization grew, a constantly increasing minority did self-directed work, individually or in small groups, indoors; these were the artisans in the skilled trades, who met the demands of growing communities. Then came the great change to the factory system through the development of power devices; this dates virtually from the invention of the steam engine.

In the second place, the industrial worker formerly knew a *whole* job, rather than a part of it; he performed a great variety of functions in the completion of his task, instead of endlessly repeating the same operation. The clockmaker made a *whole* clock, working individually, and the necessity of working out every part's relation to every other part gave the worker a mental stimulus, and, therefore, a higher mental development. The finished product was all his own; the desire for self-expression, which every man has, found an outlet through his work; and, once having served his thorough apprenticeship, he worked largely by self-direction. Under our present highly organized industrial conditions the making of a clock is subdivided into a large number of operations. Each workman in a clock factory makes piece after piece of the same kind, principally by feeding material into a machine, and why he does it he need not know and usually is not told. We are putting the brains into the machine and into the management office, and making the workman a purely automatic adjunct.

EFFECT OF DIFFERENT KINDS OF WORK ON HABIT CENTERS AND THINKING CENTERS

Now we have, broadly speaking, two types of brain centers: the lower centers controlling habits, and the higher active thinking centers. If one's work is purely automatic repetition requiring no initiative, planning, or diversion, the habit centers are developed and the thinking centers have at best a retarded growth.

In this connection it is necessary to differentiate between casually repeated useful habits of daily life which economize time, and constantly repeated automatic motions which constitute one's major work; the argument is fallacious that, because the former are good, so are the latter. The putting on of one's shoes is governed by one's habit centers; when we were learning to put on our shoes the thinking centers were being developed. Dressing, eating, walking, boarding a car, opening a door are time-saving actions of habit repeated at comparatively long intervals, differing widely in their motor forms, and used as incidental instruments to a larger self-directed action. There is a vast difference between using many habits several times a day as means to self-directed ends, and repeating *one* habit all day as an end in itself. The playing of scales on a piano becomes a habit to the skilled musician; he uses it as a means of performing a stimulating, energizing, thought-requiring production. It is a good and beneficial habit which facilitates and simplifies his performance. But if he learned the scales merely to repeat them ten hours a day, day after day, without meaning and without end, his work would become lethargizing and enervating.

It should be noted, too, that automaticity of itself does not impair one's thinking capacities. When we walk, our habit centers control the action; but we can walk and think at the same time. The evil of automatic machine-feeding is negative rather than positive, in that it requires no constructive exercise of the thinking centers, and hence develops only the habit centers. There are, however, certain types of automatic work which are distinctly injurious because they introduce other deteriorating factors. For example, if the work requires that the eyes be focused constantly at one place, if the motions of the machine before the eyes be a monotonous, rhythmic repetition, and if the

Work as Related to Modern Industrial Conditions 9

motions of the hands in feeding the material into the machine be also rhythmic and monotonous, then a deadening hypnotic effect is produced upon the mind; such is the work of a punch-press operator.

Further, automatic work, in addition to putting the thought centers into disuse and producing a lethargizing effect, is repressive of individuality. There has been developed in each of us, through the self-directed work of our ancestors in past centuries, a natural instinct for self-expression. Prior to the day of subdivided automatic operations the worker had an outlet for his self-expression in his work; now, for the automatic worker, it must come in his idle hours, and often in forms which lead to many of our most vexing sociological problems. Unexpressive (or repressive) work is unnatural work, and must incite to mental and physical protest.

MODERN INDUSTRIAL CONDITIONS

Now, we cannot reverse our present economic order of things. Work which does not require mental activity is increasing, and will continue to increase for a long time to come. The condition is here and philosophical discussion will not remove it.

RESULTS OF DECREASE OF ENERGIZING AND INCREASE OF ENERVATING WORK

The situation, then, sifts down to this: Energizing work is decreasing; enervating work is increasing. We are rapidly dividing mankind into a staff of mental workers and an army of purely physical workers. The physical workers are becoming more and more automatic, with the sure result that their minds are becoming more and more lethargic. The work itself is not character-building; on the contrary, it is repressive, and, when self-expression comes, it is hardly energizing mentally. The real menace lies in the fact that in a self-governing industrial community the minds of the majority are in danger of becoming less capable of sound and serious thought, because of lack of continuous constructive exercise while engaged in earning a livelihood.

LAWS OF THE TWO KINDS OF WORK

It is evident, then, that the general law of labor must be divided into two laws; namely, the law of energizing work, which makes for progress, and the law of enervating work, which makes for retrogression. Nearly all the work still done in the open air, where there is a dependent sequence of operation, involving planning on the part of the worker, is energizing work. Specific examples may be cited in farm work, railroad work, and the building trades. Certain work done indoors, under good conditions of light and air, is also energizing; for example, the work of a toolmaker, a locomotive assembler, and a cabinet maker. The enervating work has come through the subdivision of labor in factories, so that each worker does one thing over and over in the smallest number of cubic feet of space. This type is recognizable at once in the routine of the garment worker, the punch-press operator, the paper-box maker, and the shoe worker. On small, isolated farms, where a certain routine week by week has been established by long usage, mental development lags and the work may not be as energizing as in certain indoor occupations. In the main, however, most of the enervating work is done indoors.

Aside from the broader factors, such as climatic conditions and racial characteristics, it is safe to say that the morale of a community depends upon the kind of work it does. A rural community of about twelve thousand people, having clean political conditions, a high moral tone, few jarring families, well-kept gardens, and a good average of intelligence, is a desirable place, from the manufacturer's viewpoint, in which to locate a factory. If a manufacturer locates in such a place and employs three thousand of the men, women, and children in purely *automatic, noisy, high-speed work,* the town will change very materially in one generation. Its politics will become corrupt and its morals lax; its citizenship will lose its former mental stability and fly eagerly and earnestly from one spectacular " ism " to another; its families will be on nervous edge, with family discipline gone; its yards and houses will lose their tidiness; saloons will increase — in a word, it will become a "factory town." And what was once a good community, with a high community efficiency, and, therefore, a safe place in which to invest money, becomes a town of low community efficiency and a constant menace to the industry itself. Every detail of the town's life is affected. Religion lags, while the amusement parks thrive on Sunday; for, since the weekday work is repressive, an outlet for pronounced self-expression is demanded in the idle hours — or, to put it in another way, Nature goes on the defensive. The slowly upbuilt appreciation of the fine arts is quickly destroyed, for this cannot grow without harmony, orderly thought, and the desire to express ideals. Respect for law diminishes, for the law is put in the same class as an electrically wired strike fence. These significant changes are not the fault of the people who work; they are logical natural products of the work itself.

CHAPTER III

CLASSIFICATION OF WORK

A CLASSIFICATION of work from the most enervating to the most energizing, having in view the development of the whole man, is not only a desirable but a necessary thing in attempting to solve the problem of industrial education. Probably there is no type of work (if it may be dignified by the word *work*) more enervating than a repetitive operation of complete uselessness. Even the lowest order of mentality would rebel in time against doing a thing merely to undo it, again to do it and undo it, hour after hour, day after day. Let a man, no matter how stupid, be required to carry a stone a short distance, drop it, pick it up, carry it back to its first position, and repeat this thousands of times, forward and backward, with personal isolation added to the task — how long could he endure it before his spirit broke and his mind was overturned? If it were desired to disintegrate him speedily, the addition of foul air and nerve-racking noise would accomplish it.

It will be noted that the sheer horror of this work rises from the fact that it lacks meaning, fails to accomplish an end, and is purely absurd repetition. It is the absolute zero of work. Certain types of automatic industrial work are almost as enervating as this, the only difference being that the industrial work is not useless. But frequently the worker's only reason for knowing it is not useless is the fact that he would not be paid for doing it if it were; that, in some cases, is the full extent of his knowledge of why he is doing it. On the other hand, the most energizing work is probably that of a pure research man in science;

Classification of Work

especially where the building of apparatus and some outdoor investigation are necessary parts of his work. Between these two extremes lies the whole range of human labor.

SCALE DEVISED FOR PURPOSES OF CLASSIFICATION

For the purpose of emphasizing the different factors which make the effects of work so variable, we may devise a scale within the more usual ranges of human work, placing the most energizing at the 100 per cent point, and the most enervating at the zero point. The 100 per cent work selected is that of the locomotive engineer, because his work has the following elements:

(a) It is done in the open air.
(b) It provides a well-rounded physical development.
(c) The constant improvements in locomotive design and railway appliances generally require continuous mental development.
(d) Mental alertness is constantly required for emergencies.
(e) A comprehensive grasp of the whole interdependent scheme of transportation is essential. This firmly establishes mental coördination.
(f) The conditions under which the same run is made are never alike.
(g) The work itself — not preachments or popular acclaim — the work itself breeds in the engineer the highest quality of good citizenship; namely, an instant willingness to sacrifice himself for the lives in the train behind him. This makes for the best type of civic responsibility.

The zero point on the scale, or the most enervating work selected, is the work of a girl, in her formative years, in a steam laundry, when the following elements prevail:

(a) Supersaturated, vitiated air.
(b) Standing in a strained position.

(c) The work consisting of feeding one piece after another of the same kind at high speed into a machine.
(d) The hours of work being so long that fatigue poisons accumulate.

The scale is crude and lacks scientific accuracy. A statement, for example, that the work of a laster in a shoe factory is 40 per cent energizing would be a guess. But the purpose of the scale is not so much to arrive at a percentage as to establish some standard of actual work for the purpose of diagnosis and treatment. Three investigators, analyzing the work of a laster, might classify it as 30 per cent, 40 per cent, and 50 per cent energizing. The difference in their classifications would lead to a closer analysis, and hence to a surer treatment.

EFFECT OF WORKING CONDITIONS ON RATING

It should be noted that, where the work is done under conditions which permit the operatives to talk, without endangering them or interfering with their work, the rating is higher than where such is not the case. When we walk, our habit centers control the action, but we can walk and think at the same time. Similarly, in automatic occupations, if the motions are not too rhythmic, both of the hand and of the machine, and conversation is permitted and possible, the work is not nearly so repressive. In a certain mill, employing girls at strictly automatic work, the employees were placed facing one way, so that one operator looked upon the back of another; between adjacent operators was a small partition. This mill had to replenish its entire force each year, because of the nervous strain of the work, until the scheme was changed to a round table plan, which encouraged conversation. After this the losses were normal.

CLASSIFICATION OF WORK ACCORDING TO ITS EDUCATIONAL VALUES

Work cannot be classified by trades; for example, it could not be stated that the work of shoe workers was at a certain point on the scale. In this industry there are from fifty to one hundred and fifty kinds of work, depending upon the factory organization. In different shoe factories the same occupation will vary in its position on the scale by reason of environment. The elements whose effects determine the positions on the scale are principally the following: monotony, automaticity, noise, bad ventilation, personal isolation, posture, and fatigue.

It will be evident, then, that the problem of industrial education cannot be approached from the point of view of trades as defined by the materials used in the trades, as, for example, the wood-working trade, the iron-working trade, the textiles, or the garment-working trade. In a machine shop the punch-press operator has an enervating job, while the tool-room apprentice has a highly energizing job. In the foundry there is the same difference between the job of the molding-machine operator and that of the skilled molder. In fact, in nearly every trade, classed by materials, this wide variation in the effects of different jobs will be found. Since the problem confronting us is the relation of education to industry, necessarily we must classify work by its educational values rather than by the material used or produced.

CHAPTER IV

INDUSTRIAL EDUCATION IN THE PUBLIC SCHOOL

OBJECT OF INDUSTRIAL EDUCATION TO PRODUCE A MENTALLY AND PHYSICALLY SOUND CITIZENSHIP

IT must be remembered also that the whole human organism has been rapidly placed under new stresses by modern factory organization after centuries of more leisurely, quiet, diversified, and self-directed work; and their effects upon the kind of citizenship we are building must be a major consideration of the public school, in considering its connection with industry. Any policy of industrial education, which the public school adopts, must be built upon the rock-bottom basis of the mental and physical soundness necessary to the citizenship of a self-governing country. The object of all education is to make a good citizen, and, while the first duty of a good citizen is to earn his own living, there is his equal duty to be a good citizen in the civic sense; and it must be remembered that both duties require a sound body and a sound mind.

BENEFITS TO BE DERIVED FROM EDUCATION BY THE DIFFERENT GRADES OF WORKERS

It must not be assumed for a moment that a proper measure of production on the part of each worker is at all minimized in this argument; on the contrary, a high degree of both mental ability and manual skill in industry is affirmed as being vital to the continued industrial well-being of a community; but in some cases the school, at least, must differentiate between shaping life to industry and shaping industry to life. Initially and fundamentally, industry is a machine built to simplify the basic problem of self-preservation; but modern industry is in danger of becoming an end rather than a means. In some of its phases it controls the individual, and tends to cause him to deteriorate; it ought to be controlled by him and help to build him up. It is the old story of Frankenstein. In so far, then, as industry offers work which in itself leads to increased manual skill, continuous mental development, and well-preserved health, the school need have no hesitancy in joining hands with it in the training of workers. But, if the skill required is an endless repetition of the same simple motions, involving no mental activity on the part of the worker, and leading to physical disorders, the school could not justify itself in initiating such manual skill. The school cannot ignore, however, the fact that such work exists. It has a very definite function to perform because of the very existence of this type of work; but its function is not supplemental, it is counteractant; and ultimately its work in a counteracting way would be the most valuable work it could perform for industry. Nor will it do for the school to argue against these unfavorable conditions in modern industry. Automatic and subdivided work are here to stay, and, while many of their evils can and ought to be modified in the factory, the fact remains that they must be met by school authorities, since each year thousands of children — young men and young women — go into these enervating occupations; and the amelioration of the lethargizing effects of the work is a moral obligation which cannot be dodged.

Industry wants skilled workers. By reason of its new policy of the subdivision of labor, its need is no longer for the more broadly skilled artisans; hence, its apprenticeship system is gradually disappearing; further, because of the demand on the part of managers for greater production, the superintendents and foremen feel that they cannot be bothered with apprentices. But, because a certain amount of skill is still necessary, industry turns to the school for help.

THE SCHOOL TO SUPPLY TRAINING WHICH IS LACKING IN INDUSTRY

It is complained that the school no longer trains as it once did. As a matter of fact, the school never did train for industry specifically. The whole trouble is that industry has ceased training for itself. This training was originally very valuable education, and, since the youth of the country have been deprived of the advantages which the old apprenticeship system gave, it may be properly assumed that it is the function of the school to inaugurate such plans as will give manual training and which, at the same time, will make for mental development and sound physical health.

The public school must insist upon carrying out the prime function for which it is organized; namely, the sound mental, material, and moral advancement of the whole people.

The Problem in New York City

CHAPTER V

THE NUMERICAL SIZE OF THE PROBLEM

DISCREPANCY BETWEEN ATTENDANCE AT ELEMENTARY SCHOOLS AND THAT AT HIGH AND VOCATIONAL SCHOOLS

IN all the public schools of New York City (1909–1910) the average daily attendance (not enrollment) was 586,673. If these pupils were placed in a straight line, each one having two linear feet of standing room, the line would extend 222 miles. The average daily attendance in the day high schools was 30,252; this line would be 11 miles long. The total number graduated from all the day high schools (1910) was 2,477; the line would be about one mile long. The average nightly attendance in the night elementary schools was 27,725; the line would be 10½ miles long. The average nightly attendance in the night high schools was 9,343; the line would be 3½ miles long. The average daily attendance in the boys' day vocational school was 109. The line would stretch about one short city block. The average daily attendance (1911) in the girls' day vocational school was 360.

WHERE THE CHILDREN ARE

Employment certificates are issued by the Department of Health to children between the ages of fourteen and sixteen years. The number of certificates issued is shown by the following table:

Employment Certificates Granted

	Year 1910	First ten months, 1911
Manhattan	18,537	17,295
The Bronx	3,278	3,192
Brooklyn	11,672	12,066
Queens	2,296	2,488
Richmond	567	437
New York City	36,350	35,478

These figures indicate, in part, the size of the problem of the education of workers. The terrible school mortality from elementary schools to high school graduation class also shows that the immediate and pressing problem is to be found in store and factory and office; that is where the children are (see table, Appendix A, page 85). It is not in the school, for the majority of children who are of an age to acquire industrial training are not there.

CHAPTER VI

THE INDUSTRIAL SCOPE OF THE PROBLEM

DUTY OF THE SCHOOL TOWARD WORKERS IN ENERVATING TRADES

HERETOFORE educational efforts in industrial education have been directed almost exclusively to the more energizing trades, such as plumbing, woodworking, blacksmithing, and machine-shop work. A public school system, however, must have a comprehensive community efficiency as its objective, and from this viewpoint the machine-feeding occupations present the more serious problem. Hence, they must have at least the same amount of attention as the energizing work. If all the elements which make a citizen a good civic unit for a self-governing community are considered as the special business of the schools, then the problem of the mentally and physically enervated young worker is its major task.

THE GREAT VARIETY OF OCCUPATIONS

On this basis the industrial scope of the problem is limited only by the great variety of occupations into which the children go. A glance at the industrial directory will show that in its scope the problem is no less formidable than in its size.

Unfortunately, the 1910 census figures on occupations are not yet available. The reports of the New York State Bureau of Labor give data only for a limited number of factories in particular industries. Similarly, the recent reports of the Bureau of Commerce and Labor at Washington furnish insufficient material from selected trades. The only figures on occupations available are those being compiled by the Permanent Census Board. At this time the board's material furnishes information only for the district of Manhattan south of Fourteenth Street; this table is shown in Appendix A. That this latter is only approximately correct is shown by the following letter from the Permanent Census Board, dated September 28, 1911:

"Inclosed you will find a summarized statement of the occupations of children between fourteen and eighteen years of age, living below Fourteenth Street, as shown by the records of this office. Your request that this information be tabulated included the subdivision of these occupations into skilled and unskilled labor. The material more or less naturally divides itself into unskilled work, factory work, and what we ordinarily term the skilled labor of the trades, but failure to know the exact nature of the work done by the individual in each case makes impossible any rigid distinction or comparison, either between the various occupations of each class or between the occupations of different classes.

"I have talked somewhat at length with various people well informed on this subject — notably Professor Richards of Cooper Union — and all that I have learned tends to emphasize this conclusion. Professor Richards is particularly emphatic on this point. I am, therefore, sending you the list arranged in order of numerical importance. It seems to me that even this arrangement cannot fail to be extremely significant, as out of almost 25,000 children who are represented such a large number are engaged in casual work or 'blind alley' occupations.

"I think it is only proper to add that I believe we have not found a large number of children between sixteen and eighteen years of age who should have been listed, and possibly an equally large number between fourteen and sixteen years. Many people do not regard children above sixteen years of age who are employed, and have been employed for some time, as children, and without intentional deception they fail to include them in the statement given to the officers. These facts have developed again and again when the census has been amended.

"On the other hand, children between fourteen and sixteen years of age are omitted through a fear that something might happen to take them away from their employment, if the desired information is produced. How many there are in both these classes I am unable to say. I anticipated such a result from the start, but believe that, as the census is amended from time to time, and as we come to know those children who leave school to go to work, we can, in the course of a few years, very closely approximate the numbers actually existing between those ages.

"I think, however, you will find the list submitted nearly — if not fully — as significant as the one including all the names. We have some additional information concerning the number of positions held by the various children which possibly might also prove of service. It has not as yet been arranged, but, if needed, that could be done without any very great additional effort.

"Very truly yours,
"(Signed) GEORGE H. CHATFIELD,
"Secretary."

CHILD WORKERS FOR WHOM VOCATIONAL GUIDANCE IS NECESSARY

The table on page 85, referred to above, gives a general idea of the problem of industrial (including commercial) education which the school authorities must face in this one division of the city. Some of the occupations are fairly energizing and require no manual dexterity; for example, those of errand boys and girls, stock boys and girls, wagon boys, office boys and girls, messengers, newsboys, venders, bellboys.

It is highly probable that few of these occupations were chosen with any forethought. The child took the first job that offered simply because he wanted to go to work or was forced to work. Since these are children's occupations, by the time the worker is eighteen years old it is necessary for him to go to a higher position or seek a job with another firm. The problem for this class, therefore, is, first, one of vocational guidance, and then of collateral instruction leading to a predetermined occupation.

THE SMALL NUMBER ENGAGED IN ENERGIZING POSITIONS

Another large division in this table is made up of more or less automatic workers, such as machine operators, garment workers, paper-box makers, hat and cap workers, button makers, folders, and cigar makers.

The very noticeable feature of the table is the small number of children in highly energizing positions, such as certain departments of the printing trade, bookbinding trade, plasterers, masons, painters, decorators, carpenters, and iron workers.

CONDITIONS IN THE CITY AS A WHOLE

The statistics for Division 1 must not be assumed to represent the general condition of the city; on the contrary, certain parts of Brooklyn will show a much higher percentum of energizing trades and fewer "blind alley" occupations, while certain upper East Side districts of Manhattan may show many purely automatic and hence enervating trades. It may safely be assumed, from the State Bureau of Labor's incomplete compilations, that, when complete statistics are available, the same multiplicity of occupations will be found to prevail in the other industrial and commercial divisions of the city. It should be noted, too, that in some so-called trades there are many subdivisions; in shoemaking, for example, there are between fifty and one hundred and fifty separate and differently named kinds of work.

CHAPTER VII

PRESENT PLANS OF INDUSTRIAL EDUCATION

SCHOOLS not under the direction of the Board of Education are not included in this inquiry.

1. DAY INDUSTRIAL SCHOOLS

The city has two day industrial schools — the Vocational School for Boys (138th Street near Fifth Avenue) and the Manhattan Trade School for Girls (23d Street, east of Third Avenue).

Vocational School for Boys

The boys' school is intended for those boys who desire an education that will prepare them for industrial work as distinguished from office work. The courses offered are as follows:

A. Vocational:[1]
    Woodwork —
        House carpentry and construction.
        Cabinet making and bench work.
        Wood turning.
        Pattern making in wood.
        Use of wood milling machinery.
    Metal work —
        General machine shop practice.
        Sheet metal work.
        Forging.
        Plumbing.
        Electric wiring and installation.

[1] From a pamphlet issued by the school.

Printing —
:   Estimating costs.
    Composition.
    Imposition.
    Presswork.

B. Drawing:
    1. Mechanical —
        Working drawings.
        Isometric drawings.
        Architectural drawings.
    2. Freehand —
        Industrial design.
        Making and reading blue prints.
C. Non-vocational subjects:
    1. Trade mathematics —
        Arithmetic.
        Use of symbols (elementary algebra).
        Plane geometry as used in trade.
        Trigonometry as used in trade.
    2. English —
        Business letters.
        Reading, with oral expression.
        Drawing of contracts.
        Writing specifications, etc.
    3. Industrial history; civics.
    4. Industrial and commercial geography.
    5. Applied physics and chemistry.
    6. Simple bookkeeping.
    7. Elements of commercial law.

This school aims to bring a boy in contact with all of the various lines of industrial work mentioned under the heading "Vocational," to ascertain his bent toward any one of the particular trades offered, and to give him major work in the occupation selected. The school is not a trade school. It does not pretend to send out an artisan; it does claim to give sufficient manual dexterity and industrial insight to enable a boy to shorten materially his term of apprenticeship in a commercial shop. A good foundation is established upon which to build a real industrial apprenticeship in a commercial shop. The chief virtue of the school lies in the attraction it offers a restless and school-sick boy to continue in a less academic but vigorous school course. It renders good service as an upbuilder of the youth's mental and physical qualities, and these are necessary for industrial success.

The number of children in average daily attendance in this school during 1910–11 was 266. It will be observed, of course, that the number is almost negligible in the sum total of boys who go to work before sixteen in New York City. The type of school is good and is recommended as one of the means of attacking the problem in New York City. If additional schools are to be built, however, and if the principal objects of such schools are industrial insight and sufficient acquaintance with the various occupations to permit the wise selection of a trade, the industrial scope of the school work should be increased and should be less intensive. At the present time too much stress is placed upon manual skill in one particular trade, or one particular branch of a trade.

Manhattan Trade School for Girls

The girls' school "offers an opportunity to a girl on leaving school to learn to be a skilled workwoman in a shorter time and in a larger and more intelligent way than through trade training alone." The courses offered are as follows:

A. Vocational:
    Electric power operating —
      General operating.
      Shirtwaist making.
      Children's dressmaking and underclothing.

Present Plans of Industrial Education 31

    Women's underwear, kimonos, and dressing sacques.
Special machines —
  Hemstitching.
  Buttonhole.
  Embroidery (hand and bonnaz).
Dressmaking operating —
  Lingerie.
  Fancy waists and suits.
Straw sewing —
  Women's and men's hats.
Dressmaking —
  Uniforms and aprons.
  White work and simple white embroidery.
  Gymnasium and swimming suits.
  Dressmaking.
Millinery —
  Elementary work for assistants, improvers, frame makers, and preparers.
Novelty work —
  Use of paste and glue.
  Sample mounting, sample book covers.
  Labeling.
  Novelty work, jewelry-case and silverware-case making.

B. Art:

  Elementary —
    General courses adapted to the work of the trade departments.
  Advanced —
    Adapted to the trades as above.
  Special trades —
    Stamping and perforating.

C. Non-vocational Subjects:
  Business arithmetic.
  Business English.

Industries and textiles.
Civics.
Ethics of trade.
Cost of living.

D. Physical Education:
Physical examinations and treatment.
Exercise — invigorating, corrective, and recreative.
Talks on hygiene and health.

The average daily attendance (1911) is 360. This school is in a transitional stage; the present director having taken charge September, 1911. The girls are brought into contact with the various occupations of the vocational curriculum shown above, and the especial effort of the school is to give its pupils just enough manual dexterity and sufficient industrial intelligence to bring them to the beginning of an apprenticeship. The policy of this school is particularly sound, in that it aims to get the girls beyond the "blind alley" jobs at about $3 a week and enables them to enter an apprenticeship at about $5 a week. The school is not a trade school, and is not intended to be such. Instead of spending a great deal of time in training a few artisans, as it would if it were a trade school, it spends its efforts and funds on a much larger number of girls to start them safely in industrial life. As a prevocational school for girls, this school can be most highly recommended. A multiplication of this type of school would go far toward solving many of the problems of the juvenile female workers.

Since the children who go to this school are nearly all very poor and can afford to spend only a short time at the school, and since the work is frankly and wisely aimed to bring them to a safe beginning of an apprenticeship, only a little time is given to what are usually classed as cultural subjects. The cultural work given, however, is vitalized by connection with the distinctly vocational work.

Points for Criticism

The particular problem presented to the public school system of New York City, in so far as the girls who must go to work at fourteen years of age or thereabouts are concerned, is being admirably met in the Manhattan Trade School for Girls. The major criticism to be made of the work is really not a criticism of the school, but of the public school system, which restricts the teachers to classified lists. The widest possible freedom, in the selection of teachers for vocational work, should be given to the directors of vocational schools, since the peculiar qualifications necessary to success in distinctly vocational work cannot be determined by written examinations. A minor criticism of the work — and this is also true of the work of the boys' school — is that it is too restrictive and does not cover a sufficient number of types of occupations. This criticism is really not of these two particular schools, but of the system, which does not give adequate space and sufficient financial support to enable them to carry on the work properly.

2. THE DAY HIGH SCHOOLS

The day high schools with full manual training courses do not pretend to be industrial schools, as the following statement from the principal of Stuyvesant High School shows:

Extract from letter dated July 1, 1911, addressed to Professor Hanus by Principal Ernest R. Von Nardroff, of the Stuyvesant High School:

> "*Aims.* — Stuyvesant High School aims to give secondary instruction to young men of academic tastes, who possess a predilection for scientific, mathematical, and technical subjects.
>
> "At present the graduates of Stuyvesant generally enter higher institutions of learning in order to prepare as physicians, dentists, chemists, foresters, metallurgists,

engineers of all kinds, patent office lawyers, etc. A few graduates intend to prepare as teachers of science or as writers of science. Also a few students plan to prepare as teachers of languages and of mathematics.

"Of the graduates who do not go to higher institutions, some go into surveying; some into automobile or other manufacturing industries, as salesmen, designers, or testers; some go into architects' offices; and some go into building concerns. The great mass of boys who do not graduate at all generally enter some commercial occupation. Practically none of our pupils seek positions as bookkeepers, stenographers, or as typewriters. It is my general observation that the longer a boy not graduating remains at school the more he tends to seek employment of a scientific or technical character. Practically no boys coming to Stuyvesant High School care to enter a trade."

Principal Von Nardroff's statement is verified by the following table:

Report on Graduates of Stuyvesant High School

June, 1908—June, 1911

Amherst	1	Pennsylvania State Agricultural College	1
Brooklyn Law School	2	Pratt Institute	1
Brown University	1	West Point	1
Business Schools	1	Williams	2
Columbia University:		Cornell University:	
Mines		Civil Engineering	
Medical		Mechanical Engineering	
Chemical Engineering		Agriculture	34
Pharmacy		College of the City of New York	22
Fine Arts		Cooper Union	3
Architecture	46	Foreign Technical Schools	2
New York University:		Fordham University	1
Commerce		Long Island Medical College	3
Law		Mechanics Institute	1
Medicine		Mendell Engraving School	1
Science	9		

Present Plans of Industrial Education

New York College of Dentistry .	13
New York Law School	2
New York Normal School of Physical Education	4
New York College of Pharmacy .	3
New York Training School for Teachers	2
Total Graduates in College .	156

In Business: (Drafting, laboratory work, dental assistants, dry goods, estimating, surveying, salesmen of manufactured products)	59
In Trades	1
Deceased	3
No information	32
Total Graduates	251

3. EVENING SCHOOLS

Appendix K (report of Matthew J. Elgas, District Superintendent in Charge of Evening Schools, to Superintendent Maxwell) of the 12th annual report of the Superintendent of Schools, for the year ending July, 1910, contains a statement of the present situation in the New York evening schools with reference to industrial education, and a proposal for further development. Of the number attending the evening schools, a good proportion are foreigners, studying English.

On page 518 of the report appear the following statistics and comments:

"An analysis of the attendance gives the following interesting statistics:

High Schools

No. of pupils who attended every evening (120)	338
" " " " " 110 evenings and less than 120 . . .	1,793
" " " " " 100 " " " " 110 . . .	2,018
" " " " " 90 " " " " 100 . . .	1,594
" " " " " 80 " " " " 90 . . .	1,158
" " " " " 70 " " " " 80 . . .	1,208
" " " " " 60 " " " " 70 . . .	11,429
" " " " " less than 60 evenings	15,640

Elementary Schools

No. of pupils who attended every evening (90)	2,234
" " " " " 80 evenings and less than 90	6,050
" " " " " 70 " " " " 80	8,266
" " " " " 60 " " " " 70	10,154
" " " " " less than 60 evenings and more than one week	33,393
No. of pupils who attended one week or less	11,937

Problem of Irregularity of Attendance

"A study of these figures shows that the problem of how to improve the regularity of attendance in the evening schools is still unsolved. New York is no exception; the conditions are the same elsewhere, and in many cities even worse. It is an inherent difficulty in evening school work. I [Mr. Elgas] have already referred to one cause of the difficulty, namely, the large shifting population of the city; then again, what is too easily obtained is not properly appreciated. Another cause, no doubt, is the pressure of work at certain seasons of the year, work which sometimes continues night after night for many weeks. When the pressure ceases the pupils have lost interest and feel disheartened, and do not return. Then there are always some pupils who have little worthy ambition and who are easily carried away by the inclination rather to spend their evenings in recreation than in study. For these especially the suggestion made by you [Dr. Maxwell] on several occasions, of charging a small fee for registration, might have some effect. The fee could be returned at the end of the season if the attendance of the pupil had reached a certain standard."

Reasons for Losses in Attendance

On pages 542 and 546, inclusive, of Mr. Elgas's report are shown the subjects taught in the evening high and elementary schools. These may be subdivided into the common school branches of the day school, commercial subjects, such as stenography and typewriting, and instruction to supplement the work in the highly energizing trades.

It is unquestionable that, if a worker who does enervating work each day attempts any of the night courses offered, they will be an added burden rather than a relief or a benefit. A tired-out automatic worker cannot be blamed for having "little worthy ambition" and for "being easily carried away by the inclination rather to spend evenings in recreation than in study." It is not obvious, bearing in mind our analysis of work, that charging a fee for night-school delinquents would have any good effect. From the point of view of the promotion of good citizenship, the enervated worker is the most important for the school to consider; and consideration of his special needs must be based upon the analysis of the mental and physical results of his day's work. One of the causes underlying the losses is probably shown on page 520 in the following statement:

"With the new courses of study for the evening high school approved by the Board of Superintendents two years ago, it became necessary to prepare syllabuses for the different subjects, in order to make the work in the several schools uniform and definite. Accordingly, in December last I appointed from among the teachers twenty-one committees, consisting of from three to seven members each, to whom was assigned the task of preparing these syllabuses.

"A preliminary conference of all these committees was held on Saturday morning, December 11, at the High School of Commerce, at which I gave a brief outline of the work to be done and the lines which were to be followed.

"The committees thereafter held frequent meetings and, after completing their work, copies of the various syllabuses were sent for criticism to all the principals and teachers in the schools, and on May 12 last they were submitted for approval to the Board of Superintendents. The Board, I am happy to say, has approved them tentatively for the coming year, after which the opinion of principals and teachers is to be asked as to their practical results. In the meantime I hope that they will be put into printed form for distribution among the teachers of all the schools."

It is probable that this standardization of courses without an analysis of the daily work of students has had much to do with the losses and small attendance; the energized workers continue, the enervated workers drop out.

On page 521 the trade subjects taught in the evening trade schools are given as follows:

"The trade subjects include carpentry and joinery; cabinet making; blacksmithing; plumbing, heating, and ventilating; physics and applied mathematics; industrial chemistry; applied engineering; trade drafting; printing and typesetting; bookbinding; leathercraft; advanced dressmaking and millinery; and domestic science."

Here again is shown the tendency to provide for the energized workers only, neglecting the very important problem of the enervated workers.

Compulsory-Attendance Law an Ill-Advised Measure

It is interesting to note in this connection that there is a compulsory-attendance law, requiring all boys between fourteen and sixteen years of age to attend evening school if they have not completed the elementary day-school course. It is also stated (page 522) that it has been very difficult and, in most cases, impossible to enforce the law. Zeal for the cause of education is a good thing; but when a tired-out enervated worker, who has been compelled at fourteen years of age to take up eight or ten hours of daily grind, is forced by law to forego the recreation which Nature insists he shall have, and to sit for several more hours at night for purely academic instruction, we have evidently overreached ourselves. The classes visited, which exist because of the compulsory law, inspired no feeling but pity for the children. Some of the pupils were asleep, and all but a few of them looked fagged out; and these few, on investigation, were found to be apprentices in the machinist, bookbinding, and other energizing trades. In his 13th annual report Superintendent Maxwell recommends that compulsory night schools for these juvenile workers be discontinued. We concur in this recommendation emphatically.

Commendable Work Done

However, the night schools are doing three most commendable kinds of work, and doing them well; namely, teaching English to foreigners, teaching industrial science to those in energizing occupations, and giving instruction in dressmaking, millinery, and household science.

The foreigners' classes are lively and enthusiastic; the teachers work hard and are inspiring.

The instruction supplementing the work of energized workers — power plant operators, electricians, molders, machinists, carpenters — is, of course, night continuation-school work. The classes are composed of adults, the instruction is thorough and to the point, and the students are alert.

The women's classes are made up of garment workers and milliners seeking additional instruction for advancement in their day trades, and of wives of workingmen who want to save money by making their own hats and dresses. The latter predominate. In these classes, too, the instruction is good and the interest keen.

Rule regarding Use of Gymnasiums

One of the surprising things in connection with the night-school management is the curious rule regarding the use of gymnasiums. If a night-school principal wants to have athletic exercises he is required to obtain a special permit for each night, and must state the particular reason for each request. A good romp is often good medicine; it is one of the counteractants needed most by those whose work is done in strained physical positions or at high pressure, or which is in any other way repressive. The connection between sound health and industrial efficiency is too obvious for elaboration. Every school gymnasium should be open every night under the direction of physical directors who know the needs of those who work.

4. THE NEW YORK PARENTAL SCHOOL (NEAR JAMAICA, LONG ISLAND)

While this school is not classed distinctly as an industrial school, its work, nevertheless, is of such a character as to warrant its having a prominent place in this report. The school is organized for the care of truants and delinquents. It is without question the best prevocational school the writer has seen. In Appendix E of Superintendent Maxwell's 12th annual report (Report on the Operation of the Compulsory Education Law, by Edward B. Shallow, Associate Superintendent, page 385) is a statement on the work of this school. A part of this statement will be found in Appendix B of this report. The writer concurs in what Principal Todd and Superintendent Shallow say with regard to this school. The particular merit of the Parental School lies in the fact that every boy who stays there a sufficient length of time is brought into contact with most of the trades necessary to the maintenance of a community. The boys work one-half day and go to school one-half day in alternating sections. They do farm work, cut cord wood, do plumbing work, mend the fences, help in the cooking, build furniture, work in the laundry and the bakeshop, and, in fact, are engaged in all of the work necessary to the maintenance of a community. Careful observation is made by the teachers to obtain the boy's natural bent, and, after it has been found, his major manual work is in that particular line. But, even after his major line of work is determined, he is detailed at regular intervals to assist in various parts of the work necessary to the school's maintenance. The scheme is so devised that a boy does not obtain a high degree of dexterity in one particular line, but is brought into contact with many different types of work, and is thereby enabled to select his job more wisely when he goes to work for a living. The school develops broadly the ability to execute manually, it is man-making in its discipline, it furnishes sound mental development based, to a certain extent, on constructive work, it gives the youth an acquaintance with a number of occupations, and the military features of the school develop promptness and sturdiness without in any way being repressive. Besides doing all of this manual work, the boy receives nearly as much mental instruction as he would if he attended the usual standard school.

Desirability of Longer Period of Attendance

It is regrettable that the accommodations of the school are so limited that the children sent there can remain, as a rule, only for a maximum period of about seven months. Surely the work of taking a wayward youth and giving him training which will make him a sound industrial and civic unit is of sufficient importance to the City of New York to warrant the school authorities in immediately enlarging the Parental School. The writer is inclined to believe, after careful observation, that most of the children in the Parental School are not subnormal but supernormal. They have sharp wits, an abundance of juvenile energy, and a great deal of initiative. Their waywardness is probably due more to the fact that the public elementary schools gave no outlet for their energies, than to innate badness. The work of the school is admirably devised to set on the right track the good boy gone wrong, and to check the vicious tendencies of the bad boy; and, best of all, to give boys who would naturally become criminals an initial start in the direction of honest and industrious manhood. It is the plain duty of the City of New York to extend this work so that the school's influence may be made stronger in these wayward children through longer periods of attendance.

If the work of the Boys' Trade School and the Manhattan Trade School for Girls could be amplified to bring the students into contact with more of the occupations of the community, as the Parental School does, their efficiency would be much enhanced.

THE REAL PROBLEM CONCERNS THOSE IN ENERVATING TRADES

The sum total of the attendance in the day trade schools and in the evening trade courses does not compare favorably with the thousands of children at work. The problem is being tackled from the wrong end. The boys in energizing trades, whose minds are stimulated, and who obtain a robust physical development, do not constitute the major problem confronting New York City. But the thousands who go home every evening with fatigued muscles, nerves on edge, and brains either dulled or wearied by the day's work, whose whole being protests against any added burden of mental or physical work, and who feel the need of counteractants, such as rest, pleasure, or excitement — these present themselves to us as the great and grave problem of industrial education in New York City.

INADEQUACY OF PRESENT MEASURES FOR ITS SOLUTION

When one considers the size and the scope of the problem, as indicated above, and then considers the sum total of the work done as comprehended in the boys' vocational school of several hundred pupils, the girls' vocational school of 360 pupils, the night schools of doubtful value, and the Parental School with a few hundred, it will be evident that the problem of industrial education is in fact not being met at all. The very meager attempts so far made to meet the tremendous problem of industrial education confronting the city show that the authorities have not been alive to the needs and necessities of the great mass of working people, and, while this same indictment can be brought against practically every industrial community in the United States, and while it is most unfair to criticise in particular when the defect is general, it is true, nevertheless, that the problem is probably more vital, more complex, and more pressing in New York City than in any other city. In the few experiments under way in the day schools and in the Parental School the city has been successful, but the results in proportion to the size of the problem are entirely too meager, except in their promise, for consideration.

The Solution

CHAPTER VIII

EDUCATION PRIOR TO GAINFUL EMPLOYMENT

THE problem naturally divides into the following major and minor headings:
1. Education prior to gainful employment.
    a. Elementary training for work generally.
    b. Specific training for a given occupation.
2. Education accompanying gainful employment.
    c. The coöperative system.
    d. The continuation system.

ELEMENTARY TRAINING FOR WORK GENERALLY

The differentiated instruction which children *under* fourteen years of age should receive for further schooling and for future usefulness is discussed elsewhere (in Dr. McMurry's report on the course of study). This report deals specifically only with the vocational education of children over fourteen years of age. Under this heading, therefore, there remains the problem of general prevocational training for children over fourteen years of age.

PREVOCATIONAL SCHOOLS FOR CHILDREN OVER FOURTEEN YEARS OF AGE

The particular problem presented here is that of the child who does not intend to finish high school, who is not permitted by law to enter certain skilled trades until the age of sixteen, and who can afford to go to school only a year or two more, after which he or she must go to work. There is also the type of child who is school-sick because the book work of the schools is distasteful and even irksome; work in the store or factory is more attractive. The teacher realizes, too, that further abstract instruction is almost wholly a waste of time and effort; and it is evident also that, since the pupil will go to work within a year or two, some definite vocational training should be given him.

These are the hardest years of boyhood for which to plan. The boy, being a boy, wants to *do* things; he wants to be out of doors; he wants to build; he wants to earn money and assert a partial independence; he craves action; and he hates books. As a rule, he does not know what occupation he wants to go into, for the good reason that he does not know anything about the various occupations. When he goes to work he takes the first job offered, without any knowledge of the future possibilities of the work, and without any intelligent guidance based upon observation of his aptitudes.

These are also the hardest years of girlhood for which to plan. The first impulses to break away from home ties are apparent; the instinct for personal adornment is strong, and money is needed to satisfy it; the desire for a wider social activity is dominant, and school work is prosaic. Then there are the hundreds to whom the factory-age of fourteen necessarily means work. When the girl goes to work it is not, as with the boy, with the definite idea that factory or store work will be her life career. She expects to be married. As a matter of fact, the time spent by most girls in factory work is less than seven years; hence, the industrial-education program for girls must be modified by the domestic phases of her later life. Important as this latter phase is, however, it cannot be included in this report on industrial education.

OBJECTS TO BE AIMED AT IN PREVOCATIONAL SCHOOLS

By "prevocational school" is meant an industrial all-day school embracing as wide a range as possible of different types of occupations, with the school work arranged so that pupils can obtain acquaintance with the various occupations, and so that the teachers may observe their predilections and abilities. A high degree of manual dexterity, in any one particular occupation, is not striven for. An effort is made to ascertain the particular type of work for which the pupil is adapted, and to bring his or her skill to the point where a successful beginning of an apprenticeship is possible. These schools should formulate a broad curriculum of doing and thinking for upbuilding physically, energizing mentally, for ascertaining the natural bent of a student, acquainting him with the character of work available in industry, uncovering his limitations and defects of mind and body, and giving opportunity for the discovery of exceptional talents. In the case of the girls, it is imperative that their training be more intensive (except in the purely automatic trades; and there should be no training at all in the prevocational schools for the automatic trades) than that of the boys, because of the moral obligation of society to get the young girls more quickly to a higher wage. The present policy of the Manhattan Trade School for Girls, with sufficient amplification to embrace more occupations for girls, is a safe precedent for New York to follow in the matter of girls' vocational schools.

The writer cannot suggest a better type of prevocational school than the Parental School on Long Island. It will be contended, however, that the great variety of work offered in this school could not be duplicated in the congested districts of the city; some of it cannot, but much of it can. It is more important to note, however, that the methods and underlying principles of the parental school can be introduced into prevocational schools in different parts of the city. The same relation of work to study, which has been found so beneficial there, can be duplicated; the same methods of mental and manual coördination can be used; and the same underlying motive of a good broad practical basic training can prevail. Sound vocational guidance would naturally follow in such a scheme. Many boys who now leave school because they are school-sick would be retained for a year or two longer because the school work would appeal to their boyish instincts. The evil of a haphazard selection of an occupation would be largely avoided. The natural desire of a boy to be constructively employed on tangible things would be met, and through the meeting of this desire the efficiency of his mental equipment could be increased.

In the prevocational schools here advocated it would be the function of the directors to search out the most energizing and diversified types of work possible. The work should not be restricted to a few kinds of machines and trades, as most trade-school work is, but, as far as possible, should have the breadth and diversity characteristic of the Parental School on Long Island. The plan here proposed is merely to meet the boy as he is and not as you think he ought to be; to utilize his natural constructive tendencies for the advancement of his mental, moral, and physical sturdiness, and to start him on the career in which the talents he possesses will make him most efficient.

2. SPECIFIC TRAINING FOR A GIVEN TRADE

Trade Schools in the Enervating Occupations. — By "trade school" is meant a school which in its shops reproduces factory conditions as nearly as possible, and which aims by full-time attendance of its pupils to graduate an artisan competent to enter a trade without further apprenticeship, or at most with but a short apprenticeship.

As already stated, there are two major elements of industrial efficiency which the school may consider — manual dexterity and mental development. It has been pointed out that in the enervating occupations the continuous performance of certain monotonously repeated operations leads to a stunting of mentality. As a rule, these manual operations are easily learned; the habit can be acquired in a few days or weeks. Speed in executing them is a matter of time and temperament.

This type of work, if long continued, tends ultimately to mental retardation, which is the opposite of the second element — mental development. In the purely automatic types of work, then, the public school must choose between manual dexterity and mental development. It will choose the latter, for to initiate or to increase enervating manual dexterity would not be education. Trade schools for enervating occupations cannot, therefore, be a part of the public school system. As a matter of fact, trade schools for machine-feeding occupations have never been seriously considered by school authorities.

In the Energizing Occupations. — If trade schools in the energizing occupations are set up as the solution, and if they are as efficient as they are claimed to be, their graduates will monopolize the energizing occupations, for no employer would maintain apprentice courses if an adequate supply of skilled workers were available. It follows, then, that only those children who could afford to continue their schooling until they were sixteen to eighteen years old would get the energizing positions: the less favored ones, whom necessity or parental misguidance drives to work at an early age, would be barred from them. In effect the public school would step over into industry and close the door of the highly skilled trades to all but those who could afford to go to trade schools. The basic idea of democracy is equal opportunity, especially in the struggle for a living; and the public schools could not stand for the more favored financially and against the less favored in the field of industry.

ARGUMENTS CONCERNING TRADES TO BE TAUGHT

If trade schools are *not* efficient enough to produce skilled workers, the argument for them fails. It may be contended that even the most needy parents would send their children to such schools, and that nearly all the children would, therefore, learn good trades. This would mean a large number of artisans for a small number of jobs, with the consequent ills of overproduction; for it must be remembered that energizing work is decreasing and enervating work increasing.

[1] "Further, there remain the two tests of efficiency and economy. The ability of trade schools to turn out skilled workers has been seriously questioned; this is still an open matter. But any school which attempts to do so must throw out obsolete equipment just as a well-managed factory does. Therefore, if a trade-school policy is adopted for a large enough number of children to make any appreciable solution, the city would be compelled to make such an initial and continuous expenditure that the imagination is staggered. The advocates of trade instruction in the public school systems sometimes evade these very essential facts by saying that the more important trades only should be taught. This latter plan at once raises two very important questions:

"1. Who shall decide which are the more important trades, and how shall public support be obtained from all sources for these few trades?

"2. Are all the children to be taught a few trades, leaving all the other trades neglected, and leaving the predilections of the children out of the question entirely? Or will only a few be trained in the more im-

---

[1] "Fundamental Principles of Industrial Education." By Herman Schneider. April 16, 1909.

portant trades, and the rest be allowed to shift for themselves as heretofore?

"Should this be attempted, it would simply be a partial solution, and a very small one at that, of the whole problem of industrial education. If, for instance, we have public schools teaching the plumbing, machinist, woodworking, and molding trades, what would be the solution for all the children entering the numerous other trades?

"There is, further, the taxpayer to take into consideration. Assume that A and B are citizens in moderate circumstances, and paying about the same amount of taxes. A has a boy and a girl and B has a boy and a girl. A's boy desires to be a machinist, and the public schools will train him; A's girl desires to be a stenographer, and the public schools will probably train her. B's boy wants to be a watch repairer. Has not B the same right to demand that the public schools teach his son to be a watch repairer as A has that they teach his son to be a machinist? Shall the public school system say to B's boy: You must be a machinist, plumber, molder, or woodworker, or go without a trade training? B's girl wants to be a telephone operator. Must she learn her work without any school training?

"Is it fair for the owner of the machine shop to suggest that the telephone company train its own help, when he demands that the public schools train his help?"

INADVISABILITY OF SCHOOLS FOR TEACHING ENERVATING TRADES

In view of the foregoing it should be evident that an attempt to solve the problem by putting schools for teaching enervating trades in the public school system would not be education in any good sense. To limit trade instruction to all-day schools teaching the energizing and semi-energizing trades would result in unjust discrimination against the poorer children, who could not afford to attend an all-day school, demand a tremendous expenditure of funds, and afford but an incomplete answer to the question. The big problem would still be before us.

CHAPTER IX

EDUCATION ACCOMPANYING GAINFUL EMPLOYMENT

I. THE COÖPERATIVE SYSTEM

A HIGHLY efficient system which would be entirely beyond the resources of the city would be just as futile as an economic scheme of low efficiency. Further, the adoption of any system which might be both efficient and economical, but which would be applicable to only a small percentum of the workers, would be equally futile. In solving the problem it is fair and wise and most efficient to give mental efficiency to the thousands of children already at work. This solution means, therefore, a combination of manual work in the commercial shops with school work. There are two distinct methods of obtaining this combination; namely, the coöperative system and the continuation system.

The coöperative system is based on an agreement between a group of manufacturers and a school system whereby the manufacturers agree to institute and carry on a thorough and comprehensive apprentice course in their particular trades; and in which the school agrees to give both general and specialized instruction to the apprentices. The course of work which the student receives in the shop is scheduled by the shop and must be approved by the school authorities. The school course is devised by the school authorities. In most cases the amount of school instruction is equal to the amount of shop work. The apprentices are usually divided into two sections, which alternate with each other, for example, by weeks, so that when one section is at the shop the other is at school, and both shops and school, therefore, are always full-manned. The apprentices are paid for their work in the shop on the regular apprenticeship scale of their particular trade. The school is under no burden of expense for physical equipment, except the usual laboratory equipment. There are no practise shops in the school to teach manual dexterity.

Work of the Coördinators

In order that the work of the school may be definitely coördinated with the work of the shop, a separate set of teachers is sometimes employed. These may be called coördinators. The shop coördinator is a teacher well versed in shop practise. He spends every morning at the school and every afternoon in the shops. His function is to make a direct coördination of the work of the shop with the instruction of the schools.

The coördinators make a careful study of each shop, and devise organization charts showing the path which a student can most profitably follow through the shop. In addition to the shop chart, a chart is made for every individual student which indicates how closely this path is followed, and why there are deviations, if any. These charts are the result of closely observed experiment on the part of the schools and the shops, and are worked out by conferences between shop coördinators and shop superintendents.

Practical Success of the Coöperative System

It has already been demonstrated in this country by actual experiment (at Fitchburg, Mass.) that the average young man can acquire an energizing trade and do nearly as much school work as that required in a high-school course by four years of coördinated half-time work in each. It has also been demonstrated that the alternation by weeks of student-apprentices causes no annoyance or inconvenience to the school or to the shop. Experience to the writer's knowledge has covered work in drafting rooms, chemical shops and laboratories, machine shops, pattern shops, building trades, boiler shops, outdoor work of railroads, track, signal, bridges; courses are now being inaugurated in cloth fabric factories, grocery stores, and a variety of other occupations. Under this system the student is assured a complete and thorough apprenticeship, since it is the function of the school to see that breadth and thoroughness of training are maintained in the commercial shop work. No girl or boy may be exploited by overzealous foremen, as the visits of coördinators prevent this. Alternating periods and alternating sections are, of course, not necessary in this system, since this is not the distinguishing feature of the plan. The essential factor is the agreement on a broad and thorough apprenticeship, with coördinated schooling, carefully checked and maintained in actual operation by the school authorities. The various coöperative plans (at Fitchburg, Mass.; Solvay, N. Y.; Lewis Institute, Chicago) have demonstrated that the course is commercially profitable to the manufacturer and to the student, and economical for the school.

2. THE CONTINUATION SYSTEM

Under the continuation system, the employer releases his employees of school age for a period of time (e. g., one-half day or a whole day) per week to attend the public schools for definite mental instruction. The instruction given at the school is entirely under the control of the school authorities; but the school authorities have no control whatever over the shop work. The manufacturer does not agree upon any definite apprenticeship course, his only obligation being to send the workers to school for a definite number of hours per week, with or without pay. This type of school is in extensive operation in Germany, and a few have been started in this country. It has been shown in

America by actual experiment (in Cincinnati) that a worker in the energizing trades who goes to school for one-half day per week, on pay, is a better producer per week than if he does not go.

Specific details of these systems will now be cited.

CHAPTER X

THE COÖPERATIVE COURSE IN DETAIL

TRADES TO WHICH THE SYSTEM HAS BEEN APPLIED

THE coöperative system has been applied so far only to the more energizing trades, which have fairly definite plans and periods of apprenticeship, as, for example, the machinist trade, molder trade, pattern-maker trade, plumber trade. This is because the coöperative system contemplates a deliberate life choice of a trade on the part of the youth; and no boy or girl deliberately selects an automatic machine-tending job as a life job. It is selected haphazard, usually from necessity; nearly always the immediate cash return is the only consideration. Coöperative plans have been devised for the more automatic trades, where these are the only trades available and where deliberate selection of a more energizing trade is out of the question; but these are just being put into operation, and hence there are no data to show whether or not they are better adapted to these trades than the continuation scheme.

Coöperative courses vary in detail to meet local and trade conditions. Specific details of coöperative courses follow:

DURATION OF COURSE AND METHOD OF OPERATION

The duration of the course is determined by the length of time required for a thorough apprenticeship plus the necessary coördinated schooling — usually four years. The first year is sometimes spent wholly in school and the next three years in alternation weekly between shop and school. In some cases, the full four years are spent in weekly alternation.

The manufacturers take the student-apprentices in pairs, so that they have one of the pair always at work, and likewise the school is provided with one of the pair. Each Saturday morning the boy who has been at school that week goes to the shop in order to get a knowledge of the job on which his alternate is working, so that he will be ready to take it up Monday morning, when the shop boy goes to school for a week.

1. SHOP WORK

Shop work in the commercial shop consists of instruction in all the operations necessary to the particular trade.

The apprentices receive pay for the weeks they are at work, at the prevailing apprentice rates.

A candidate is usually given a trial period of one or two months preceding the opening of school, and if he likes the work and shows aptitude for the trade he takes the course; otherwise he drops out, and, if he chooses, takes up some other trade. Thus the boy is given an opportunity to find himself. During this probationary period the coordinators observe the apprentices at their work, and talk to their foremen and fellow-workmen to ascertain their aptitudes.

Answers to Objections to the System

Objection is frequently made on the part of shop owners to the coöperative system on the assumption that alternating sets of students would cause confusion and inconvenience to the shop organization. Experience, covering a period of four years (at Fitchburg, Mass.; Solvay, N. Y.; and Chicago, Ill.), shows that this assumption is false. Emphasis is placed on this detail because it is the principal objection raised by shop superintendents when the coöperative system is proposed. The owners of shops using the coöperative system are a unit in stating that, while trouble of this kind was anticipated, it has never developed. Shop managers have also opposed the plan for the reason that the withdrawal of a student-apprentice would leave the machine idle every other week. The actual operation of this system shows that there can never be more than one odd man in the shop, since if there are two odd men they can be combined into a new pair. Actual experience has taught that there is no difficulty in taking an odd boy from one shop and pairing him with an odd boy in another shop. In a few weeks they are alternating as smoothly as the original pair. If two boys are at different stages of development in their shop work, the smooth adjustment of their new combination is brought about through intensive instruction, by the coördinator, of the less advanced one.

Diversification of Work a Necessity

The layout of the apprenticeship courses in the shop contemplates an advancement from the simple to the more complex work at the various machines and throughout the necessary departments to make a well-rounded mechanic. From the point of view of the shop, any particular kind of work has only one value; namely, the practical value of material production. From the point of view of the school, there is the added value of the mentally stimulating character of the work. For example, repetition of work in turning out certain pieces on a lathe increases the manual dexterity of an operator, and hence his output. This makes for increased production, and hence the longer the period of time the student is on a given job the greater his output. A shop superintendent, looking at an apprentice course solely from the point of view of production, would emphasize the necessity of long periods of time on repeated processes. From the point of view of the school, however, the long period of time on such processes would destroy, to a certain extent, the educational value of the apprentice course. The school would contend that a great variety of work on the lathe, with less immediate production, would, in the long run, insure a better mechanic; not only because his mental stimulation would be greater, but because he would be competent to perform a greater variety of tasks. Further, when the work is more diversified, the coördinator obtains many more practical problems, illustrating mathematics and science in the school. It will be evident, then, that in many cases the shop course will be a compromise. As a matter of actual experience in coöperative courses, it has been found that, after a year or two of operation, the shops are entirely willing to accept a plan of diversified work, as suggested by the coördinator, largely because the mental results of the greater variety of operations are clearly evident during the apprenticeship period; and nearly every shop superintendent knows that the ability to think, on the part of the mechanic, is as fundamentally essential as his immediate ability to do.

Feasibility of the System in Automatic Trades

The arrangement of shop work in the more automatic trades is a much more difficult task. Skill in a machine-feeding shop is almost entirely a matter of manual dexterity. The shoe manufacturer, for example, who has subdivided the operations of his factory into over fifty distinct kinds of work, contends that knowledge of all the operations of a shoe factory is not necessary for the worker doing any particular piece of work. He points out that the skill in one process can be obtained in a short time; that knowledge of previous or subsequent processes in the making of a shoe is not essential to the quantity of production in any particular part of shoe making; that most of his workers are usually girls to whom the immediate cash return is more important than a thorough knowledge of the trade; and that the seasonal, the competitive, and the manually simple conditions in his industry make impossible and unnecessary a scheme of apprenticeship similar to that in carpentry, plumbing, or bookbinding. It is probably true that the immediate production of the shop would not be increased, and might be decreased, by a broad apprenticeship system, similar to that devised for the energizing trades mentioned, since in his trade manual dexterity is the essential thing. There are no experimental data by which to confute this argument. The theoretical contention that a broad knowledge of shoe making, on the part of, say, a laster, would increase the laster's interest in his work and make for stability of employment; lead to the discovery of better equipped and more intelligent foremen and forewomen; tend to counteract the lethargizing effects of the work; and, by shifts from one type of work to another, decrease the physically debilitating effects of nervous tension, monotony, and automaticity, can only be determined by experiment. The value to industry of a high general intelligence and sounder moral tone, which would come through the operation of such courses, must be counted in favor of a coöperative system. Unfortunately the immediate cash value of these conditions to an employer is not apparent on his books, and hence they are frequently considered by him as social questions with which industry has nothing to do.

It will be evident, then, that the introduction of coöperative courses into the more automatic trades will not be so feasible as in the more energizing trades. When, however, industry counts as an asset the broader intelligence and greater stability so necessary to a self-governing industrial community, and turns to the public schools for assistance, the actual planning of a shop scheme for automatic workers will not be a matter of great difficulty.

2. SCHOOL WORK

Since the student reports at school every other week, a repetition of school work is necessary. What was taught to "section one" last week must be taught to "section two" this week. This does not add to the expense of instruction, since in all public school work the classes are divided into sections, and it is no more expensive to teach one section Monday of last week at 9.30 and another on Monday of this week than to teach two sections at 9.30 every week. More intensive work is possible for the week the student is at school because of his alternation of mental and physical work. Four years of experience with the coöperative system at different schools have established the remarkable fact that nearly as much work can be done in a year's time under the coöperative system as in a year's time under the regular system. It must be remembered, however, that this experience has been gained by coöperation with energizing trades. It cannot be assumed that similar conditions would prevail in coöperation with enervating trades.

Application of Present Courses to Coöperative Classes

School curricula and methods of instruction will always be a subject of controversy, and the application of present school courses to coöperative classes will depend upon how the present classes are taught. If, for example, the science and mathematics courses are concretely coördinated with tangible things, they will need little or no revision. If the non-scientific subjects are themselves coördinated and made vital, no essential changes will be necessary in them. The only difference will be in the added value of more direct application of the sciences and mathematics to the worker's daily task, and the closer connection of the non-scientific subjects — such as history, civics, and geography — to modern industrial activity.

Connecting Instruction with Industry

Practical exemplifications of theory are brought to the school from the shop by the coördinator and by the apprentices themselves; and in a short time the regular teachers are sufficiently interested to get into closer touch with the industrial and other broader community activities — to be coördinators to a degree, also. For example, if a coöperative course for silk workers were in operation, the students' attention would be called to the fact that different patterns and qualities of silk are used in different countries, and even in different parts of the same country; that the pattern of silk which would sell in Brazil would not sell in Iowa. The students would be shown that this was due to a difference in the life, the customs, the tastes of the people, and that these in turn were a result of historical development and geographical location. The relation of silkworm culture in different countries to physiography and geography would be used to vitalize further these subjects. A course in chemistry, for example, in the case of a silk worker, would emphasize the connection of chemistry to industry through simple dye experiments, while in the case of the machinist apprentice simple metal analyses would be used. This would not mean the abridgment of a course, but the general interest in chemistry would be stimulated through specific applications to the occupations of the students. The connection of instruction in English with industry, through the necessity of writing good business letters, making accurate shop reports, and describing shop processes, is too evident for elaboration.

Courses in Department Stores

In certain coöperative courses, however, the time allotted for school work would not permit much more than strictly technical courses. In a department store, for example, the clerks are not busy until ten o'clock in the morning. A store can get along easily with one-half its clerks from eight to ten o'clock. The force is divided into two sections, one of which receives instruction this week from eight to ten o'clock, while the other section is working; the following week the sections are changed about. In this particular instance, the students do not go to the public schools; the teachers go to the store. It is evident that it is easier to transport twenty teachers than to transport a large number of student-clerks. A number of rooms in the store, such as carpet rooms and lace rooms, are set aside during these two hours for the class work, the chairs being removed at ten o'clock, and sufficient space being reserved for any business which may be necessary up to that time.

It is contended by department-store owners that salesmen should know the psychology of salesmanship, and have a fairly expert knowledge of the things they are selling. They should receive, besides, a certain amount of general education. The salesmanship and the more general subjects are taught by selected teachers employed by the public schools. In order to teach the practical end, the following method has been adopted: Consider, for instance, the shoe department. If one pair of shoes costs $1.85 and another pair costs $1.95, the salesman should know where the difference of ten cents' value lies. Let us assume that this particular department store buys shoes from a firm in Brockton, Mass. When it makes its next contract for shoes, it will insist that the firm selling the shoes send an expert demonstrator to its store to explain in detail all the different successive operations in shoe making and all the different elements which make differences in cost. The tanning firm from which the shoe manufacturer buys his leather will be required to send to the store an expert who will exemplify practically to the students the different grades of leather in a hide, methods of preparation, and why one kind of leather is used in one part of a shoe, and another in some other part of a shoe. It has been found that the shoe manufacturers will very gladly enter into any scheme of this sort. He would, in fact, be a very shortsighted manufacturer who would not. This same general idea is followed in all the other departments, such as jewelry, linen, silk, and furniture.

CHAPTER XI

THE CONTINUATION SCHOOL IN DETAIL

USE OF THE SYSTEM AS APPLIED TO BOTH ENERGIZING AND ENERVATING TRADES

THE continuation system is applicable to all trades, both energizing and enervating. The whole problem in the continuation school is the careful planning of the mental instruction so that it will best supplement the work done in the commercial shop. It will be evident that this mental instruction must vary widely for different trades, and must depend primarily upon how energizing or enervating the shop work may be. As the work approaches the 100 per cent point on the scale of energizing and enervating work given earlier in this report, the school work involves more of the science underlying the trade. For example, the carpenter apprentice will be taught practical mathematics, mechanics, simple stresses, reading of blue prints, the proper use and care of tools, etc. As the work of another occupation approaches the zero point, and becomes more enervating, the supplementary school instruction would not be the same as that in the energizing job; for, in many cases this would be an added burden to an overstrained organism rather than a relief. In certain high-speed repetitive processes the instruction would be planned solely to counteract the lethargizing tendencies of the work itself. Even in the same trade the instruction would vary. For example, in a factory making leather articles, one worker may be merely an automatic machine operator, while another may be on highly skilled, artistic, and energizing work. In a machine shop, the work of a punch-press operator is monotonous and lethargizing, while the work of a boy in the toolroom is highly energizing. The course of instruction given to the automatic worker would be planned solely for the stimulation of his active thinking centers. On the other hand, the skilled leather worker or toolroom apprentice would have a school course devised to teach him the science underlying his work, and to give him industrial intelligence broadly. In the case of the automatic workers, there would probably be no increase in output at first, whereas in the case of the skilled worker, the increase in production and the decrease in losses would be apparent.

SCHOOL WORK OF THE ENERGIZING WORKER

The continuation course for the toolroom apprentice would include shop mathematics, the elements of mechanism, and writing and spelling, as they are found to be necessary; history and geography taught broadly by their connection with definite industrial conditions existing in the trade of the student; and, finally, courses in hygiene and civics, having to do primarily with the intimate details of city life in connection with the apprentice's daily health, transportation, pleasures, rights, and privileges.

METHOD OF TREATING THE AUTOMATIC WORKER

The school work of the automatic worker presents a more difficult problem. It seems to be a well-established fact of observation that these workers have a pronounced natural craving for things that are lively and immediately interesting. They patronize the moving-picture show, the amusement parks, the dance halls; they want excitement. This is strictly in accordance with what scientific investigation would lead us to expect. The repression of the day's work prompts Nature to go on the defensive, and hence the demand for something which is not dull, prosaic, or according to a fixed schedule as the daily task is, and as formal school work would be. To the unthinking, school courses which would take advantage of the opportunities offered by moving pictures; which would be especially devised to have life and color; which would counteract the dull monochrome of monotonous work; and which would be so informally conducted as not to give the feeling of compulsion, would not be education and hence an unnecessary waste of public money. Nevertheless, the school authorities are confronted with the fact that they must institute such courses, or that certain types of workers will get the same stimulation by more vicious means. The school authorities must face the fact that the usual methods of instruction will fail dismally for workers whose daily work is repressive, monotonous, and automatic, and that they must devise plans which will meet the situation which is now being met largely in a commercial way for private gain. Fundamentally the school must make the same appeal to the same desires as the shows and the parks do. This statement will probably be read with abhorrence by many school men; nevertheless, unless the situation is met in this way it will not be met at all, so far as the schools are concerned, and, since the object of education is the fostering and maintenance of good citizenship, the public schools have, in the case of the enervated worker, a very important problem. They have to take this worker as they find him with his intense and very human desire for self-expression after daily repression, and, whether they want to or not, they must take their cue from those who are meeting this desire in a commercial way. The vicious features incident to satisfying this craving can be eliminated, and the work so organized that it will be mentally stimulating, physically upbuilding, and morally beyond criticism.

The statement that the continuation-school courses for the girl at the zero point must be the most brilliant and healthful pleasure courses possible may excite ridicule; but if the critic will attempt to formulate some other scheme for, say, the laundry worker mentioned in the scale of work, which will not be an attractive and pleasurable course, he will find absent the one thing necessary for the success of the plan; namely, the presence and interest of the worker.

COURSES IN PART CONTINUATION AND IN PART COÖPERATIVE

There is a type of course which may be partly continuation and partly coöperative. These courses are in operation in seasonal occupations. For example, in the building trades in Chicago the apprentices work full time during the spring, summer, and fall; during the winter months, when building work is slack, by agreement between the school and the employers they attend school for certain definite instruction. These courses may be usually classed as coöperative, inasmuch as the apprenticeship during the nine open months is agreed upon, and, during the three winter months of school, the theory of the work is taught.

Particular emphasis is placed upon the fact that no hard and fast rule for the operation, in detail, of the coöperative and continuation courses can be made. There is in each case a most efficient plan, alike for the employer and the employee, and each type of occupation must be studied to ascertain the proper relative amounts of shop and school work, time of attendance, curriculum, and methods of instruction.

CHAPTER XII

HOW TO INAUGURATE CONTINUATION AND COÖPERATIVE SCHOOLS — COMPARATIVE ADVANTAGES OF THE TWO PLANS

CONTINUATION courses may be instituted in two ways: First, by compelling the employer to send his working people, between certain age limits, to the schools for a certain percentage of the working hours; and, secondly, by inducing the manufacturer to consent, voluntarily, to coöperation with the public schools. Since the coöperative system involves an agreement on the part of the employer to maintain a thorough apprentice system, it can hardly be made compulsory by legal enactment unless laws governing apprenticeship are also enacted.

COMPULSORY SYSTEMS

Under the first plan the establishment of the continuation school may be made mandatory by legislative action, both for the employer and for the public school. In Wisconsin, for example, the employer is required to send all his employees, between the ages of fourteen and sixteen, for five hours of instruction per week during working hours. The law further limits the number of working hours per week for these children to forty-eight, including the five hours for school. As a result of this law, some children were discharged, either to be idle or to go back to school for full-time instruction, until the law permits them to work full time in the shops. The Ohio law makes it obligatory on the part of the manufacturer to send his employees between certain ages for a certain amount of instruction to such continuation schools as the public school authorities may deem it advisable to inaugurate. This plan permits the school to make a study of industrial conditions and to govern the solution accordingly. Under either compulsory system the manufacturer has no option in the matter of sending his employees between certain ages to the public schools.

THE VOLUNTARY SYSTEM

The second system, in which action by the manufacturers is voluntary, is as a rule harder to put into operation. The manufacturer must be convinced that four or eight hours per week in the school-room will so increase the efficiency of the young worker that production will not decrease; at least that it will not decrease sufficiently to make it a serious element in his competition with another employer who does not permit his employees to attend school. In some industries, a competitor would suffer for a time and possibly indefinitely by the continuation system if he adopted it and his competitor did not. This is especially true of an industry such as the shoe industry, where a large number of juveniles are employed. In the voluntary schools, so far inaugurated in this country, practically all of the employers in a given industry have agreed mutually to send their juvenile workers to school for a certain period of time; but they are still at a disadvantage in competing with outside employers whose workers work full time. In the more highly skilled trades, such as the machinist trade and the pattern-maker trade, it has been shown (in Cincinnati) that the production per week is not lessened by the attendance at school. In the Cincinnati plan, the employers pay the apprentices for the time at school just as if they were at their machines.

ENLISTING THE INTEREST OF MANUFACTURERS

In the voluntary system, the first problem confronting the school men desirous of establishing continuation or coöperative courses is to get the interest of the manufacturers in each particular trade. In nearly every line of industry the employers usually have an organization with a secretary and a central office. Through this secretary the manufacturers are approached by letter, by individual visits, and by meetings, to obtain their consent to some form of industrial education for their employees. In nearly every case it will be found that there are enough employers who appreciate sufficiently the seriousness of modern industrial conditions to give the school men a good-sized class. To begin continuation courses requires a considerable amount of study in order to determine the time of day and time of week that the children are to be taught, the subject-matter to be given, and the method of its presentation; and there is always the difficult matter of finding the proper teachers. This latter difficulty has been used as an argument against both the coöperative and the continuation systems. It can be used, however, with equal force against the day trade school, for, as a matter of fact, the trade-school teacher ought to be more efficient than a continuation-school teacher, since he has both theory and practise to teach, while the continuation-school teacher has only the theory to teach.

USE OF THE TWO SYSTEMS TO MEET VARYING CONDITIONS

It will be seen, then, that the formation of coöperative and continuation schools is a slow process, if efficiency is to obtain; and that in many cases legal enactment is not necessary for their inauguration. Of course, there may be localities in which conditions are such that no manufacturer would coöperate with the schools voluntarily, or there may be certain groups of manufacturers in certain trades,

— for example, in the seasonal trades, — none of whom would consent to the plan. Under these conditions, the compulsory system is necessary.

FACTORS DETERMINING WHICH KIND OF SCHOOL TO ESTABLISH

The second broad question to settle is as to the type of school, whether coöperative or continuation. From a manufacturer's viewpoint, the coöperative scheme offers the advantage of keeping his machine full-manned all the time. Actual experience has demonstrated, as heretofore stated, that there is no conflict, confusion, or commercial loss arising from the working in alternate weeks of two groups of workers; but, again, the coöperative system contemplates a broad and thorough apprenticeship in the store, shop, or office. Manufacturers in favor of specialization are sometimes opposed to this phase of the system. Then, again, the number of children who can afford to go to school and to shop on the half-time plan is limited; so that, aside from other considerations, both plans will have to be inaugurated. Generally speaking, it will be found that the coöperative courses will be more easily organized in the energizing trades. It will be argued that the coöperative courses, therefore, are subject to the same fundamental objection that applies to the full-time trade school, and that the more favored will therefore possess the energizing trades. A little analysis will show this to be fallacious. In the first place, a coöperative system is applicable, with a well-arranged apprenticeship, to the enervating trades, and, in the second place, if a worker cannot afford to enter the coöperative course the apprenticeship in the commercial shop is open to him just the same; and, further, at a later date, when his wages are higher, the coöperative or continuation courses are always available. The continuation scheme will be more largely used than the coöperative system because the bread-and-butter necessities will make it the only feasible plan for a large number. The coöperative scheme presents the better combination of a good apprenticeship, coördinated instruction, and a more advanced mental development.

From the point of view of the school, the coöperative course is much more difficult of operation than the continuation course. It requires a careful analysis of shop work in order to perfect a proper arrangement of the apprentice course, necessitates a carefully built internal organization for the coördination of theory and practise, and demands constant care and attention to insure its smooth operation. Unlike the usual public school course, it cannot be started in September and allowed to run more or less by its own momentum until June. The executive work of a coöperative course requires daily attention to a variety of details, just as any business does. But it has the unquestioned advantage of placing a swift and sure check on the efficiency of the instruction given in the school, and inevitably it leads to a comprehensive revision of many of the science and mathematics courses as they are now taught. In fact, this check on the efficiency of school instruction is one of the most valuable features of the coöperative course from the school man's point of view.

ADJUSTMENT OF VIEWS OF MANUFACTURERS AND OF SCHOOL MEN

Briefly, then, in choosing between coöperative and continuation courses the decision will largely be determined by the relative poverty of a community, the attitude of the manufacturers (assuming no legal enactment) to the inauguration of thorough apprenticeships, and the willingness of the schools to undertake a varied and more exacting system of instruction.

One evening, about a year prior to the writing of this, the writer had two addresses to make in New York City. The first was before a body of school teachers and the second before a group of manufacturers. Before going on the platform at the school teachers' meeting he was requested not to make an attack upon trade schools; that is, schools which attempt to teach trades by full-time attendance at school. He was told that, while it was generally conceded that the coöperative and continuation schools are the most efficient, they are not possible in New York City because the employers would not agree to their adoption, and that hence only the trade school was possible there. At the second meeting, after an explanation of the coöperative and continuation systems, there was a lively discussion in which one manufacturer after another expressed a desire for these courses — but said that they were impossible because of the attitude of the school people. The attitude of the schools was assumed to be one of antagonism toward industry and a lack of concern toward industrial efficiency.

PRACTICAL ACHIEVEMENT OF HIGH IDEALS

It has been conclusively demonstrated that the school and shop can work together if the one common ground will be the mutually safe ground of the mental, physical, and the moral advancement of those who work. This will seem to the superficial critic a too ideal basis on which to do business in this day and generation. He will probably agree that it is a nice scheme to have in mind, but an impossible one upon which to operate. There is but one satisfactory answer to this; namely, that the thing is being done and is being done satisfactorily.

Conclusions

CHAPTER XIII

CONCLUSIONS CONCERNING INDUSTRIAL EDUCATION OF CHILDREN — IMPROVEMENTS IN PRESENT FACILITIES RECOMMENDED

WE recommend —

1. CONTINUATION SCHOOLS

That day continuation schools be inaugurated for those children who are forced to go to work when the law permits them to do so. The occupations into which the children go should be carefully studied so that the curricula of these continuation schools may be wisely devised. It must be observed that the school work of the enervating occupations must differ from the school work of the energizing occupations in that it must counteract the influence of the work rather than supplement it. If it be found that employers are opposed to this plan, we recommend that a compulsory-continuation-school law be submitted to the General Assembly of the State of New York. This law should require the employer to send children to school not less than four hours per week during the daytime wherever the public school system inaugurates such schools. Because of the size of the task involved, the law should not make it mandatory for the schools to establish continuation courses all at once; but when they are established the law should make it mandatory for the manufacturers to send the children to them for day instruction.

2. COÖPERATIVE COURSES

That coöperative courses, to a limited extent, be inaugurated. Coöperative courses contemplate an agreement between the public school authorities and commercial shops, whereby the shop authorities agree to establish thorough, old-fashioned apprenticeship courses, subject to the approval of the public school authorities; the public school agrees to inaugurate special courses intended to give the apprentice in the commercial shop a well-rounded mental training. As a rule, students in the coöperative courses should spend alternate periods of time (for example, alternate weeks) in the schools and in the commercial shops. The student-apprentices in the coöperative course are divided into two alternating sections, one being at the school while the other is at the shop; in this way both school and shop are always full-manned.

3. DISCOURAGEMENT OF TRADE-SCHOOL SYSTEM

We are opposed to the introduction of the trade-school system for industrial education. By "trade school" is meant a school which in its shops reproduces factory conditions as nearly as possible, and which attempts, by full-time attendance of the pupil, to graduate an artisan competent to enter a trade without an apprenticeship, or at most with a very short apprenticeship. If this type of school were put into operation, it is obvious that it could not be applied to enervating occupations. If it were applied only to energizing occupations, and if enough schools were built to supply the energizing trades with artisans, the result would be that the children less favored financially would be compelled to take the enervating occupations; for the manufacturer would discontinue his apprenticeship course if the public schools supplied him with artisans. In effect, then, the public school would be going over into the field of industry and closing the door of the energizing occupations to the poorer children, who could not afford to continue in the trade school until they were seventeen or eighteen years old. In addition to this, the trade school would solve only a very small part of the problem, because it would reach only a relatively small number of children and serve only a limited number of occupations. Carried to its logical conclusion, it would oversupply the market in the skilled trades.

4. PREVOCATIONAL SCHOOLS

That the curricula of the Boys' Vocational School and of the Girls' Vocational School be broadened to embrace a larger number of *types* of occupations. These schools are really prevocational schools. We further recommend the inauguration of free vocational schools patterned after the Boys' Vocational School and the Girls' Vocational School after their curricula have been amplified.

5. ENLARGEMENT OF THE PARENTAL SCHOOL

That the Parental School (Long Island) be enlarged so that children sent there may remain a greater length of time. The school is now so crowded that the benefits obtainable for the children are restricted by the time each child is allowed to remain.

6. INVESTIGATION OF PRESENT CONDITIONS OF CHILD WORKERS

That a comprehensive survey be made showing the number of girls and boys employed in different occupations; whether the work is energizing or enervating; whether it is juvenile work only, or whether it offers good permanent employment; whether or not it is seasonal; together with the usual vocational statistics on wages, home conditions, reasons for leaving school, etc. This survey should include an analysis to ascertain when the workers could best be released from their work to attend school.

7. ENACTMENT OF A COMPULSORY EDUCATION LAW

That a compulsory education law be enacted for juvenile workers similar to the Ohio law, which makes the introduction of day continuation schools optional with the school authorities, and which makes attendance mandatory when the schools are put into operation.

8. ABOLITION OF ELEMENTARY NIGHT SCHOOLS

That the elementary night schools, operating under the compulsory education laws, be abolished.

9. COÖPERATION BETWEEN THE SCHOOL AND THE SHOP

That a propaganda be undertaken through neutral sources to awaken all the elements of the city to the serious educational problem growing out of the city's work. We do not make specific recommendations on *how* the school and the shop shall be brought into coöperation. We do recommend, however, that a system of advisory boards, consisting of representatives of employers and employees in the various occupations, be inaugurated to assist in bringing them together.

Appendices

40.000
8000

APPENDIX A

OCCUPATIONS OF CHILDREN BETWEEN 14 AND 18 YEARS OF AGE IN DIVISION I, COMPRISING DISTRICTS 1, 2, 3, 4, 5, 6, 7, AND 9, BEING THAT PORTION OF THE BOROUGH OF MANHATTAN LYING SOUTH OF FOURTEENTH STREET, ARRANGED IN ORDER OF NUMERICAL IMPORTANCE

Occupations Having More than 100 Workers

Occupation	Boys	Girls	Total
Errand Boys and Girls	2,733	358	3,091
Housework	....	1,812	1,812
Clerks	1,367	378	1,745
Machine Operators	385	1,050	1,435
Office Boys and Girls	857	271	1,128
Salesmen and Saleswomen	416	456	872
Packers and Wrappers	306	554	860
Helpers	557	215	772
Not Known	481	277	758
Feather and Feather Dusters Workers	25	685	710
Messengers	663	46	709
Workers on Shirtwaists and Shirts	49	643	692
Bookkeepers	201	409	610
Stock Boys and Girls	310	298	608
Outer Clothing Workers	117	427	544
Tailors, Tailoresses, etc.	375	139	514
Seamstresses	....	509	509
Stenographers and Typewriters	59	367	426
Paper-Box Makers	134	282	416
Hairdressers and Makers of Hair Goods	57	330	387
Millinery	8	346	354
Wagon Boys	340	....	340
Neckwear	33	286	319
Artificial Flowers	27	275	302

86   *Education for Industrial Workers*

Occupation	Boys	Girls	Total
Dressmakers	....	299	299
Printers	235	....	235
Embroidery Workers	27	201	228
Hat and Cap Workers	63	108	171
Underwear Workers	9	162	171
Confectioners	41	127	168
Newsboys and Newsgirls	163	5	168
Drivers	162	....	162
Bookbinders	52	99	151
Servants and Waiters	33	100	133
Leather Workers	78	46	124
Venders	114	6	120
Button Makers	56	54	110
Folders	12	96	108
Cleaners and Sweepers	85	22	107
Bottlers	35	70	105
Jewelers and Dippers	90	14	104
Box Makers	43	60	103
Fur Workers	59	42	101
	10,857	11,924	22,781

Occupations Having Less than 100 Workers

Occupation	Boys	Girls	Total
Cashiers	19	76	95
Paperhangers, Plasterers, Plumbers	86	....	86
Telephone Operators	20	53	73
Electricians	68	....	68
Machinists	64	....	64
Tobacco and Cigar Makers	23	38	61
Corset Makers	4	56	60
Card and Picture Mounters	17	41	58
Suspender and Garter Makers	27	31	58
Pressmen and Lithographers	56	....	56
Barbers	55	....	55
Outdoor Workers (Unskilled)	48	6	54
Grocery Clerks	38	16	54
Belt Makers	23	30	53
Musicians	30	20	50
Umbrellas	26	23	49
Combs — Ornaments	24	25	49
Bootblacks	49	....	49
Dyers and Cleaners	49	....	49

Occupations of Children

Occupation	Boys	Girls	Total
Hats, Bonnets, and Frames	13	28	41
Masons, Painters, and Decorators	40	....	40
Trunks	27	11	38
Braiders, Tassel and Fringe Workers	16	22	38
Brass Workers	30	4	34
Glove Makers	3	31	34
Mechanics	33	....	33
Carpenters	32	....	32
Bellboys and Hallboys	32	....	32
Bakers	25	4	29
Agents and Collectors	22	3	25
Corset Examiners	3	22	25
Elevator Boys	25	....	25
Laundresses and Laundry Workers	6	19	25
Butchers	23	....	23
Pipemakers and Polishers	19	4	23
Instructors	6	15	21
Workers on Novelties	5	15	20
Telegraph Operators	11	9	20
	1,058	634	1,692

Occupations Having Less than 20 Workers

Occupation	Boys	Girls	Total
Nurses and Nurse Girls	....	18	18
Lamp Shade Workers	13	4	17
Gold and Silver Workers	16	1	17
Engravers	17	....	17
Government Employees	15	1	16
Amusement Performers	8	6	14
Iron Workers	12	....	12
Window Dressers	12	....	12
Wood Polishers	11	1	12
Liquors, etc.	11	....	11
Compositors	11	....	11
Artists	6	4	10
Rubber Workers	8	1	9
Upholsterers and Mattress Makers	7	2	9
Sorters	2	6	8
Solderers	8	....	8
Hostlers	6	2	8
Bead Workers	....	8	8
Blacksmiths	7	....	7

Occupation	Boys	Girls	Total
Designers	2	5	7
Stonecutters	6	....	6
Musical Instrument Workers	6	....	6
Dentists	6	....	6
Coppersmiths	6	....	6
Draftsmen	5	....	5
Models	2	3	5
Photographers	4	....	4
Librarians	4	....	4
Buyers	2	2	4
Embossers	2	1	3
Manicurists	....	3	3
Sawyers	3	....	3
Ushers	3	....	3
Conductors	1	....	1
Lamplighters	1	....	1
Weavers	1	....	1
	223	69	292

Summary

	Boys	Girls	Total
Occupations having more than 100	10,857	11,924	22,781
Occupations having less than 100	1,058	634	1,692
Occupations having less than 20	223	69	292
Total			24,765

APPENDIX B [1]

THE NEW YORK PARENTAL SCHOOL

The New York Parental School was opened for the reception of pupils on May 19, 1909. Therefore, more than one full year has elapsed since we began the various activities of this school.

No better demonstration of the wisdom of establishing the school need be given than is presented in the character of the class-room work, and in the mechanical and agricultural work performed by the boys.

The school-room work is organized on the departmental plan. Each teacher is a specialist in his or her line. Boys who were truants or incorrigibles largely because of a dislike for school-room routine develop a remarkable liking for study and recitation. Principal Todd says: "Many of the boys not only ask if they may go to school all day, and work outside during their recreation periods, but frequently and voluntarily ask to be put back a grade when they find that the grade they are in is too difficult. One of our boys while in the Jamaica Hospital asked to have his history and arithmetic sent to him so that he might study and save time while away from school."

Boys in all grades from 1A to 4B, inclusive, attend school in the morning, and all those in grades 5A to 7B, inclusive, attend in the afternoon. The time not spent in school is devoted to work in the shops, to farm and garden work, to helping in the bakery, the kitchen, and the laundry, to cleaning the cottages, and to practise in the band. Ample time is allowed for recreation, military drill, and athletic sports. The boys rise at six o'clock in the morning and retire at eight at night and sleep soundly after a day of study, work, and orderly routine. From all this entirely new habits are acquired. From six months to a year of this kind of life makes a remarkable change in the great majority of the boys. "All our staff who have had experience in other institutions for correcting the unfortunate juvenile delinquent quickly note," says Principal Todd, "the ease with which our boys respond to the discipline of the school, and the marked change in all the boys after they have been in the school a short time, also the great difference in the boy's view of his responsibility when he is eligible for parole or discharge." Only about $5\frac{1}{2}$ per cent of the paroled boys have been returned for violating parole.

In noting the effect of the discipline of the Parental School, it may be interesting to refer to one case in particular. A boy of twelve years of age from

---

[1] From Appendix E, Report on the operation of the Compulsory Education Law, to Superintendent William H. Maxwell, by Edward B. Shallow, Associate Superintendent, July 11, 1910.

South Brooklyn was committed by the court, about two years ago, to a private institution on a charge of truancy and incorrigibility. At the end of one month he escaped from the institution; was captured after several weeks, escaped from the institution a second time, was recaptured and transferred to the Parental School, from which he escaped within a month. After a period of a few days he was caught, returned, and disciplined. Finally he told the principal that he would submit to the regulations of the school. This boy was paroled in due time, and has been attending a school near his home regularly for many months past. The desire for right conduct is such among the boys that any attempt at disobedience, or the use of profanity or vulgar language on the part of any one, is immediately reproved and condemned.

The industrial work at the Parental School for the past year not only shows excellent results, but is a certain indication of the greater things that we can accomplish in this line when the facilities of the school are enlarged.

The tailor shop, which has been in operation only since January 1, 1910, shows good results in addition to the knowledge of the trade which the boys are learning. The following is a statement of the articles made, with their market value and the cost of production:

214 summer uniforms made, value $4.00 each	$856.00
Repairs to winter uniforms	100.00
	$956,000

Cost of Production

1,000 yards khaki, at $.143 per yard	$143.00	
Linings, threads, shears, buttons	206.81	
Salary of instructor	300.00	
		$649.81
Net profit		$306.19

In the laundry 26,702 articles have been washed during the year for the Parental School, the Brooklyn Truant School, the Manhattan Truant School, and the Hall of the Board of Education.

The market value of this work is	$5,760.05
The cost of operation was	1,379.16
Total saving over amount of previous contract price for work	$4,380.89

The following is a statement of the market value of the products of the bakery, the amount produced, and the cost of production:

Value of total product, bread, rolls, cakes, pies, etc.	$4,885.31
Cost of production, wages, flour, miscellaneous	3,981.80
Net profit	$903.51

The New York Parental School

From May, 1909, to June 21, 1910, 55,967 loaves of bread and 13,183 rolls were baked and distributed among the truant schools.

Our Parental School farm has supplied the Manhattan Truant School with vegetables, the Brooklyn Truant School with potatoes and green corn, and the School Ship with two loads of vegetables. The market value of all the products of the farm for the year ending May 31, 1910, was $2,529.78.

The School band has been in existence about four months. No boy in this organization knew anything about any musical instrument when enrolled in the band. To-day the boys can play creditably about twenty selections. They appear twice a week at flag drill. Their playing in the village of Flushing at the celebration on July 4th was one of the enjoyable features of the day.

In the plumbing shop the boys are receiving much practical instruction. This instruction includes nearly all elementary work in the trade. They have learned to cut, thread, fit, and solder pipes, and have made many repairs to the plumbing in the building, besides laying a line of pipe from one of the cottages to the temporary stables.

I am pleased to report that we have secured the services of a practical printer, and now the printing shop is in operation.

The work in the carpenter shop is about all that is done in a regular elementary school under the course of study. The boys from the shop will soon be ready to build a fence along the rear of the farm.

The net weekly cost per capita for the instruction and maintenance of boys in the Parental School, based on an average attendance of 177, for the last year was $3.85. In this the cost of coal, maintenance of plant, and operating the power house are not included, but the cost of provisions purchased in 1908 before the school was opened is included.

The following is a statement of changes in registration at the school during the year:

Admitted during the year		437
Returned on broken parole		25
		462
Paroled	233	
Discharged	26	
In hospital	7	
Transferred to other institutions	2	
Escaped, not returned	2	
		270
Register, June 1, 1910		192

Respectfully submitted,
EDWARD B. SHALLOW,
Associate City Superintendent, and Committee on Compulsory Education.

Index

INDEX

Apprenticeship system, the early, 6; disappearance of, due to subdivision of labor, 17; under the coöperative system, 55–57, 59 ff.; under the continuation system, 57–58, 67–70.

Arithmetic, business, courses in, in industrial schools, 29, 31.

Art, courses in, in Manhattan Trade School for Girls, 31.

Attendance, at public schools in New York City, 21; at evening schools, 35–39; desirability of longer, at New York Parental School, 41–42.

Automatic labor, under modern industrial conditions, 7; effect on habit centers and thinking centers, 7–8; repressive of individuality, 9; effect of introduction of, into a community, 10–11; most enervating forms of, 12, 13; relation of the public school to conditions produced by, 16–17.

Automatic trades, question of feasibility of coöperative system in, 62–63.

Automatic workers, treatment of, under the continuation system, 68–70.

Blind alley occupations of child workers, 26.

Bookkeeping courses in Vocational School for Boys, 29.

Boys, Vocational School for, New York City, 28–30, 81; number in attendance at Vocational School, 30; at New York Parental School, 40–42, 89–91; why prevocational schools are needed for, 47–48; occupations of working, 85–88.

Building trades, a form of energizing work, 10.

Cabinet making, an example of energizing work, 10.

Chatfield, George H., letter by, quoted, 24–25.

Chemistry, applied, courses in, in Vocational School for Boys, 29.

Chicago, coöperative system in, 57, 60.

Child workers, occupations, 23–27, 85–88; investigation of conditions, desirable, 81–82.

Cincinnati, continuation system in, 58, 72.

Citizenship, effect of enervating work on, 11; production of a mentally and physically sound, the object of industrial education, 16.

Civics, courses in, in Vocational School for Boys, 29; in Manhattan Trade School for Girls, 32.

Classification of work, 12 ff.; scale devised for purposes of, 13–14; effect of working conditions, 14; according to its educational values, 15.

Commercial law, elements of, taught in Vocational School for Boys, 29.

Community advancement through industrial efficiency, 3.

Compulsory-attendance law, an ill-advised measure as applied to evening schools, 38–39.

Compulsory systems, used in continuation schools, 71–74; advised for New York City, 82.

Continuation system, the, 55, 57–58; description in detail, 67 ff.; use as applied to both energizing and enervating trades, 67–68; school work of the energizing worker, 68; method of treating the automatic worker, 68–70; how to inaugurate, 71 ff.; enlisting interest of manufacturers, 73; factors determining advisability of establishment, 74–75; conclusions concerning inauguration of, 79.

Coöperative system, the, 55 ff.; practical success of, 56–57; trades to which applied, 59; duration of course and method of operation, 59–60; shop work in the, 60–63; feasibility of, in automatic trades, 62–63; school work, 63–66; how to inaugurate, 71 ff.; enlisting interest of manufacturers, 73; factors determining advisability of establishment, 74–75; conclusions concerning inauguration of, 80.

Coördinators, work of, 56–57.

Cost of living, courses in, in Manhattan Trade School for Girls, 32.

Courses in prevocational schools, 28–29, 30–32, 49.

Department stores, coöperative courses in, 65–66.

Diversification of work, necessity for, 61–62.

Drawing, courses in, in Vocational School for Boys, 29.

Dressmaking, courses in work connected with, in Manhattan Trade School for Girls, 30, 31.

Education, classification of work according to its values for, 15; industrial, in the public school, 16 ff.; object of industrial, as concerns citizenship, 16; industrial, in New York City, 28–33; prior to gainful employment, 47 ff.; inadvisability of, for enervating trades, 53–54; accompanying gainful employment, 55 ff.; the coöperative system, 55–57, 59–66; the continuation system, 57–58, 67–70; courses in part continuation and in part coöperative, 70; conclusions concerning industrial, 79 ff. *See* Schools.

Efficiency, industrial, elements determining, 3.

Electric power operating, courses in, in Manhattan Trade School for Girls, 30–31.

Elementary schools, average daily attendance, 21; discrepancy between attendance at, and that at high and vocational schools, 21–22; attendance at evening schools, 36; abolition of evening, recommended, 82.

Elements determining industrial efficiency, 3–4.

Elgas, Matthew J., report on evening schools, 35–38.

Employment certificates, number issued, 21–22.

Energizing work, 6; decrease of, under modern conditions, 9; law of, 10; examples of, 10; highest form of, 12–13; of child workers in New York City, 25–26; education in, in prevocational schools, 50; trade schools in, 51; use of continuation system as applied to, 67–68; effect of trade-school system on apprentices, 80–81.

Enervating work, 6–9; increase of, under modern conditions, 9–10; law of, 10; examples of, 10; chiefly done indoors, 10; deadliest form of, 12; duty of the school toward laborers in, 23; of child workers in New York City, 26; effect on attendance at evening schools, 37; problem of treatment of boys and girls in, by the schools, 42–43; trade schools for, 50–51; use of continuation system as applied to, 67–68; effect of trade-school system on apprentices, 80–81.

Enervating trades, inadvisability of schools for teaching, 53–54.

English, business, courses in, in industrial schools, 29, 31.

Ethics of trade, courses in, in Manhattan Trade School for Girls, 32.

Evening schools, New York City, attendance at, 21, 35–37; trade subjects taught, 38; the compulsory-attendance law, 38–39; commendable work done, 39; rule regarding use of gymnasiums, 40; recommendation concerning, 82.

Factory system, changes in industrial conditions with introduction of, 6–7.

Farm work, an example of energizing work, 10.

Fitchburg, Mass., operation of coöperative system at, 56, 57, 60.

Index

Geography, industrial and commercial, courses in, in Vocational School for Boys, 29.

Germany, continuation system in, 57.

Girls, Manhattan Trade School for, 30–33; average daily attendance at Manhattan Trade School, 32; need of prevocational schools for, 48; occupations of working, 85–88.

Gymnasiums, rule regarding use, in connection with night schools, 40.

Habit centers of the brain, 7; effect of automatic work on, 7–8.

Health element in industrial education, 3.

High schools, New York City, average daily attendance at, 21; industrial education in, 33–35; attendance at evening schools, 35.

History, industrial, courses in, in Vocational School for Boys, 29.

Humphries, Alex., article by, cited, 5 n.

Hygiene and health, talks on, in Manhattan Trade School for Girls, 32.

Hypnotic effect of certain forms of automatic work, 8–9.

Individuality, automatic work repressive of, 9.

Industrial education, object of, 3–4, 16; in the public school, 16 ff.; present plans in New York City, 28 ff.; in evening schools, 35–39; at New York Parental School, 40–41, 89–91; problem of, of those in enervating trades and inadequacy of present measures for solution, 42–43; solution of problem of, by prevocational schools, 47 ff.; the coöperative and continuation systems, 55–76; conclusions concerning, 79–82.

Industries and textiles, courses in, in Manhattan Trade School for Girls, 32.

Industry, early alliance of mental training and, 6.

Inefficiency resulting from inaction, 6.

Laundry work, a low grade of enervating work, 13–14.

Law of work, the, 5–6.

Locomotive assembling, an example of energizing work, 10.

Locomotive engineer, a high class of energized worker, 13.

Manhattan Trade School for Girls, New York City, 30–33; criticism of work, 33; a safe precedent to follow in girls' vocational schools, 49; broadening of curriculum advised, 81.

Manual dexterity, element of, in industrial education, 3.

Manufacturers, problem of enlisting interest of, in continuation or coöperative courses, 73; attitude of, a factor in determining establishment of coöperative or continuation school, 74; adjusting views of school men and, 75–76.

Mathematics, application of courses in, to coöperative classes, 64.

Mental development, importance as an element in industrial efficiency, 3; former alliance of industry and, 6; the aim of industrial schools, 51.

Metal work, courses in, in Vocational School for Boys, 28.

Millinery, courses in, in Manhattan Trade School for Girls, 31.

Night schools, average attendance at, 21. See Evening schools.

Novelty work, courses in, in Manhattan Trade School for Girls, 31.

Occupations of child workers in New York City, 23–25, 85–88.

Ohio, compulsory continuation-school law in, 71–72.

Parental School, New York, industrial education at, 40–41; a good type of prevocational school to follow, 49–50; enlargement of, advised, 81; description of work, 89–91.

Physical education, in Manhattan Trade School for Girls, 32.

Physics, applied, courses in, in Vocational School for Boys, 29.

Politics, relation between enervating work and, 11.

Index

Prevocational schools, 28 ff.; why needed, 47–48; what is meant by, 49; objects to be aimed at, 49–50; energizing and diversified types of work necessary, 50; broadening of curricula advised, 81.

Printing, courses in, in Vocational School for Boys, 29.

Railroad work, an example of energizing work, 10.

Recommendations concerning improvement of facilities for industrial education in New York City, 79–82.

Repetitive work. See Automatic work.

Repressive work, unnaturalness of, 9.

Salesmanship, coöperative courses relating to, 65–66.

Schneider, H., articles and book by, cited and quoted, 5, 52–53.

Schools, function of, in supplying elements of industrial education not furnished by industry, 3–4, 18; industrial education in public, 16; discrepancy between attendance at elementary, and at high and vocational, 21; duty of the, toward workers in enervating trades, 23. See Industrial education.

School work under the coöperative system, 63–66.

Science, application of courses in, to coöperative classes, 64.

Shallow, Edward B., report on Parental School, quoted, 89–91.

Shop work under the coöperative system, 60–63.

Solvay, N. Y., coöperative course at, 57, 60.

Special machine courses in Manhattan Trade School for Girls, 31.

Stuyvesant High School, aims and work of, 33–34; report on graduates, 34–35.

Subdivision of labor under modern conditions, 7.

Thinking centers of the brain, 7; effect on, of automatic work, 7–8.

Tool-making, an example of energizing work, 10.

Trade mathematics, courses in, in Vocational School for Boys, 29.

Trade Schools, prevocational schools distinguished from, 49; what is meant by, 50, 80; in the energizing occupations, 51; trades to be taught, 52–54; discouragement of system, and reasons, 80–81.

Trades of child workers, New York City, 23–25, 85–88.

Vocational courses, in Manhattan Trade School for Girls, 30–31.

Vocational School for Boys, New York City, 28–30; criticism of work, 33; broadening of curriculum advised, 81.

Vocational schools, discrepancy between attendance at elementary schools and that at, 21–22; desirability of inauguration of free, 81.

Voluntary continuation-school system, 72.

Von Nardroff, E. R., letter on work of Stuyvesant High School, 33–34.

Wisconsin, compulsory continuation-school law in, 71.

Woodworking courses in Vocational School for Boys, 28.

Work, basis of the instinct for, 5; natural law of, 5–6; laws of energizing and of enervating, 10; dependence of morale of a community upon kind done, 10–11; classification of, 12 ff.; scale devised for purposes of classification, 13–14; effect of working conditions on rating, 14; classification according to its educational values, 15.

GOVERNMENT HANDBOOKS

WORLD BOOK COMPANY announces the publication of a new series of college textbooks, to be called "Government Handbooks."

The editors of the series are David Prescott Barrows, Ph.D., Professor of Political Science and Dean of the Graduate School in the University of California, and Thomas Harrison Reed, A.B., LL.B., Assistant Professor of Government in the University of California.

The series will consist of small, clearly-written books, each treating of the political and administrative organization of a modern government. It is the intention to provide a handbook for each of the European countries and one on the government of American dependencies.

The authors of the different volumes will be men who combine thorough training in the subject with personal acquaintance with the country and the governmental system described.

In form the books will be compact — of a size to slip conveniently into the student's pocket. Each volume will have maps and illustrations wherever such are necessary, and will contain also a select, explained bibliography.

Volumes already in preparation are: *Government of American Dependencies*, by Dr. David Prescott Barrows; *Government and Politics of Great Britain*, by Thomas Harrison Reed; *Government and Politics of the German Empire*, by Dr. Fritz-Konrad Krüger, of the Department of Political Science, University of California; *Government and Administration of Prussia and the Federal States of the German Empire*, by Dr. Herman G. James, Adjunct Professor of Government, University of Texas.

School Efficiency Series
Edited by PAUL H. HANUS, of Harvard University

"One of the most noteworthy undertakings in professional education of the century."—PROFESSOR C. H. JOHNSTON, *University of Illinois.*

FRANK P. BACHMAN. Problems in Elementary School Administration. *Cloth, $1.50*

FRANK W. BALLOU. High School Organization. *Cloth, $1.50*

S. A. CURTIS. Standards in Arithmetic. *In press.*

ELLWOOD P. CUBBERLEY, FLETCHER B. DRESSLAR, EDWARD C. ELLIOTT, J. H. FRANCIS, FRANK E. SPAULDING, AND LEWIS M. TERMAN. The Portland Survey. *Cloth, $1.50*

CALVIN O. DAVIS. High School Courses of Study. *Cloth, $1.50*

EDWARD C. ELLIOTT. City School Supervision. *Cloth, $1.50*

HENRY H. GODDARD. School Training of Defective Children. *Cloth, $.90*

PAUL H. HANUS. School Efficiency: A Constructive Study. *Cloth, $1.20*

FRANK M. MCMURRY. Elementary School Standards. Instruction: Course of Study: Supervision. *Cloth, $1.50*

ERNEST C. MOORE. How New York City Administers Its Schools: A Constructive Study. *Cloth, $1.50*

HERMAN SCHNEIDER. Education for Industrial Workers. *Cloth, $.90*

FRANK V. THOMPSON. Commercial Education in Public Secondary Schools. *Cloth, $1.50*

WORLD BOOK COMPANY
YONKERS-ON-HUDSON, NEW YORK
CHICAGO   ATLANTA   DALLAS   MANILA